HOUSEHOLD MANAGEMENT FOR **MEN**

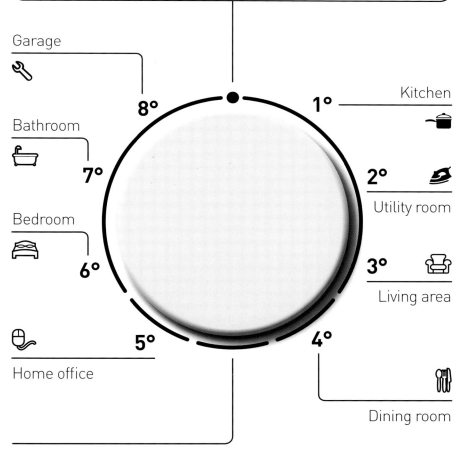

Garage

8°

Bathroom

7°

Bedroom

6°

Home office

5°

1° — Kitchen

2° — Utility room

3° — Living area

4° — Dining room

The Groundbreaking Guide
to Domestic Duties
Revised and Expanded Edition

APPLE

Contents

Introduction
The Art and Science of Household Management   6
What to Do When   8
Which Room Are You In?   10

Kitchen

Chores and No-nos   14
Kitchen Utensils: Use or Pose?   16
Whose Turn to Wash the Dishes?   20
Kitchen King or Kitchen Slave?   22
Refrigerators and Freezers   24
Ovens, Hobs and Microwaves   26

Treasure, Trash, Recycle   28
What's in Store?   30
Food Facts   32
First Aid and Safety   34
How it Works: the Microwave   36

Utility Room

Chores and No-nos   40
The Laundry Affair   42
Loading the Machine   44
Handwashing   46

Stain Solutions   48
Ironing Out Your Problems   50
The Washing Machine   53

Living Area

Chores and No-nos   56
De-junking Your Space   58
Dusting   60
Washing and Wiping   62
Stain removal   64

The Fireplace   66
Caring for Fabrics and Textiles   68
Floors without Flaws   70
Vacuuming   72
How it Works: the Vacuum Cleaner   74

Dining Room

Chores and No-nos   78
Table Preparation   80
Dressing the Table   82
Feeding and Watering Guests   84

Good Mixers   86
How to Do it:
Carving a Whole Chicken   88

Home Office

Chores and No-nos 92
Mountains to Molehills:
Paperwork Gets the Chop 94

How it Works:
Houseplants and Their Owners 96
Pets in the Office and at Home 98

Bedroom

Chores and No-nos 102
Bediquette 104
The Bedroom Routine 106
Closet Encounters 108
DIY Sewing Skills 110

Dress Sense 112
Domestic God in the Bedroom 114
The Domestic God's Routine 116
Guest Who's Coming to Stay 118
How it Works: Suitcase Savvy 120

Bathroom

Chores and No-nos 124
Top-to-toe Hygiene 126
Keep it Clean 128
Toilet Tactics: Flushed with Success 130

The DIY Spa 132
Tips for Top-to-toe Relaxation 134
First Aid Kit 136
How it Works: Soap 138

Garage

Know Your Car: Exterior 142
Know Your Car: Interior 144
Basic Car Kit 146
Tool Box Essentials 148
Basic Maintenance and Repairs 150
Under Pressure 152
Liquid News 154
I Can See Clearly Now 156

Shampooing Your Car 158
Troubleshooting Q&A 160
Ten-minute Road Check: Car 162
Understanding Your Wheels 164
Basic Bike Kit 166
Blke Maintenance and Repairs 168
Tyre Trouble 170
Ten-minute Road Check: Bicycle 172

The Art and Science of Household Management

L et's start with a few little-known but interesting facts. Household management is both a science and an art; it uses both sides of the male brain and is a practical and spiritual exercise – practical because it establishes order, hygiene and safety within the home environment; spiritual because it makes you feel more comfortable and secure within your own four walls (plus rather pleased with yourself). Even better, housework is also an aerobic exercise that allows you to flex your muscles and push your weight about at home without annoying people.

Housework is not dull, boring or a waste of leisure hours that could be better spent in front of a television or at the bar. It saves time, creates order out of chaos, burns calories and makes you sexier. Are you more interested now? Read on.

Men, when questioned about how much housework they do, often reply: 'Not my department,' 'Far too busy at work,' 'What's the point? It always looks the same five minutes later,' and 'Do you reckon Hercules did the dusting?' However, in our fast-changing world, increasing numbers of men share the household chores or, indeed, assume full responsibility for them. The dynamics are changing. Real men do housework – it's a fact. And real men get rewards.

Household Management for Men demonstrates how to approach household tasks positively and effectively, how to schedule, organize and execute tasks efficiently – just like any other job that lands in the daily in-tray – and shows how to enjoy a similar sense of achievement and fulfillment. Some jobs are more rewarding than others: dusting, like filing, can pile up and stare you in the face for some time without any major repercussions, but neglecting the kitchen sink or the laundry basket will lead to instant inconvenience. However, just think how great you feel when the filing tray is empty. It's the same with housework. And you haven't got the journey home afterwards.

This book is aimed at a fairly wide audience – male students, young and not-so-young working men, whether single, married or in partnerships, stay-at-home men, both novices and experienced home managers, together with all the women out there who want to pass on the art of household management to their menfolk, whatever their age or previous knowledge. Some readers will be new to household management, others may have

DOMESTIC GOD

Look out for the Domestic God icon if you want to fast-track to the heart of the matter (or that of your partner).

a little or even a lot of experience. They can derive some satisfaction from already having a few techniques and tips under their belt. Beginners will soon get the hang of things and move speedily from the nursery slopes to intermediate status. By page 176, all of you will be experts in the art and science of household management and ready to tackle a few off-piste tasks.

Rewarding times

We all need to feel congratulated or pampered from time to time, particularly when we have faced a challenge and successfully tackled it. Make sure you reward yourself (if nobody else is going to do it for you) by patting yourself metaphorically on the back and treating yourself to something that makes you feel good – a new book, CD or DVD, a massage, or a bottle of good wine. Tell someone what you've done. You are feeling better already.

QUESTIONS AND ANSWERS

Have a go at this quick questionnaire to find out the answer. If you get more questions right than wrong, you are not a know-it-all. You need this book badly. Answers are at the back by the way (page 144), but no cheating.

HOW OFTEN SHOULD YOU CLEAN THE BATH?

a) twice a week
b) once a month
c) when someone comes to stay
d) when there's an R in the month
e) didn't know you had to

HOW OFTEN SHOULD YOU LAUNDER YOUR BEDLINEN?

a) twice a month
b) twice a week
c) when you have a 'sleepover'
d) when your mother comes to stay
e) when your dog refuses to spend the night with you

HOW LONG SHOULD YOU GENERALLY LEAVE AN OPENED JAR OF FOOD IN THE REFRIGERATOR?

a) a couple of days
b) a couple of weeks
c) a couple of months
d) until it walks out on you
e) until your partner finds it

WHY SHOULD YOU REMOVE DUST REGULARLY FROM SURFACES?

a) it gets up your partner's nose
b) there is never enough to write your whole name in
c) it is full of dead dust mites and can cause allergies
d) it spoils the view on the television screen
e) you don't need to – just turn the lights down

HOW WOULD YOU DESCRIBE YOUR BEDROOM?

a) a sanctuary
b) a storeroom
c) a shop window
d) a no-go area
e) a scandal

WHICH ITEMS OF CLOTHING ARE CURRENTLY RESIDING IN YOUR LIVING ROOM?

a) a pair of socks and a sweater
b) one sock and one pair of boxer shorts
c) all your footwear
d) none at all – hard to believe
e) most of your wardrobe

IS YOUR DOG MORE HYGIENIC THAN YOU?

a) yes
b) no
c) it's a close shave
d) about the same
e) I don't have a dog

WHEN DID YOU LAST EMPTY THE TRASH?

a) last night
b) last week
c) last month
d) don't know where it is
e) never

What to Do When

Don't let the very thought of housework overwhelm you, just like a huge work project upon which you cannot get started. Ease yourself into it and do a little each day. Don't wait until things get completely out of control before tackling them – tasks will take twice the amount of time and be half as effective. To do it properly you need a system, a routine and a schedule. 'Diarize, prioritize, realize' is a good mission statement – it works just as well at home as on the time management course and in the office

First things first

Individuals should assume responsibility for their own clutter. Taking ownership of a problem is half way to solving it. Admitting to ownership of a pair of odorous socks under the sofa is the first step on the road to removing, washing, folding and finding them a good home. Don't upset people by de-junking their possessions without consultation. It would be like reading their post and dumping it without their knowledge or consent. Set a time schedule for the 'house de-junk' and stick to it.

If some tasks are going to take more than a few days (e.g. clearing an attic groaning with possessions, unopened packing cases, lots of trash, some treasure and mountains of dust) you will need to come up with a few long-term goals rather than immediate ones.

A little every day goes a long way

You will feel so much better when you get up in the morning if you have cleared up after your evening meal, taken the dirty dishes into the kitchen, washed and stored them, tidied the living area and sorted out your laundry and clothes for the next day. Equally, on returning from a hard day's work at the office or in the library, the feel-good factor for you and your housemates or partner goes up dramatically if the place looks tidy and clean. It is welcoming and nurturing – it makes you feel better. Even cavemen felt better when the cave looked more like a home than a butcher's shop.

Mess attracts mess – it's a fact. Three lonely and unwashed plates by the sink are quickly joined by three potential mates – they reproduce easily and soon you have a little family. If someone else can leave dishes unwashed, why can't you? Hold on a minute, though – what if someone pops round unannounced – your boss, friend or potential romantic interest perhaps? How impressed would they be to find the house in a total mess? Romance can be hard to kindle and sustain amid empty beer cans and the unappealing, pungent remains of last night's takeout. The smell of stale food is a highly effective passion killer. Underwear that has hitchhiked into the living area in less than pristine condition doesn't even bear thinking about.

Weekly wonders, monthly miracles

If you ask your mother or grandmother about the weekly routine that used to operate in her household, she may well tell you that certain tasks were performed on a particular day. For example, in many households Monday was usually washing day and Saturday baking day in the first half of the twentieth century. However, with the advent of modern technology and a change in the profile of domestic and working life, such traditions are rarely followed today. For some people, evenings and weekends are the only opportunities to do their major shopping and more time-consuming weekly or monthly tasks. Whatever applies to your own situation, establishing and sticking to a weekly schedule really does work. You could do much worse than follow in your grandmother's footsteps and start the week with the laundry and ironing. Monday is often a quiet night on the social front and you should feel energetic and refreshed from the weekend. Wash your bedlinen and towels on Monday evening, and in between filling and emptying the machine, you can vacuum, then iron your clean but unpressed shirts.

The three little words that work magic in the general context of the home are Time and Motion (I Love You works wonders too, in its place). Have a look at the list of weekly tasks and decide what suits your schedule and best copes with the demands of your home. When it comes to the monthly jobs, look in your diary and choose a time when your work and social life look less hectic than usual and dedicate a few days to the tasks. Write it in your diary, buy some stickers for the calendar, put a note on the fridge, enter the information into your computer or phone – and stick to the schedule.

Establishing a routine

Look at the situation holistically. See the bigger picture. Consider all the jobs that have to be done and create a list or chart that divides them into four headings: annually, monthly (or quarterly), weekly and daily. For those already reaching for the 'too hard' basket here's a working model:

CHORE CHART:

ANNUALLY:
- Venture into and clear out: attic/garage/ basement/cupboard under the stairs
- De-junk the wardrobe, throwing out clothes you have not worn in the past 9-12 months
- Tidy and sweep garage
- Pull out refrigerator and oven to clean behind and under them
- Wash blinds
- Shampoo carpets
- Deal with tax paperwork
- Clean ceilings and walls
- Clean duvets, doonas, quilts and blankets

MONTHLY:
- Clean oven (OK, quarterly)
- Dust blinds and shades
- Turn mattresses (OK, quarterly)
- Wash mirrors
- Launder mattress and pillow covers
- Clean windows
- Give fans a quick dust (ceiling and freestanding ones, not your admirers)
- Check supplies in larder and freezer
- Edit and tidy videos, CDs and books

WEEKLY:
- Do inventory of refrigerator and pantry for fresh staple supplies
- Buy food and household products
- Check supplies of vital items (toilet paper, washing powder, shampoo, etc.)
- Dust surfaces in main rooms
- Change towels and bedlinen (twice a week is OK)
- Clean bathroom (sink, bath, shower, toilet)
- Do ironing
- Check, clear and do interim clean of refrigerator
- Wash bins thoroughly
- Vacuum all rooms
- Pay bills and file paperwork
- Replace kitchen cloths with clean ones (2-3 times a week)
- Sort out recycling supplies

DAILY:
- Personal hygiene (see page 128)
- Make bed
- Hang up and sort clothes for laundry
- Tidy floors and surfaces
- Clean sink, bath and toilet, checking and replacing supplies
- Recycle old newspapers
- Remove clothing from living area
- Empty bins
- Tidy and wash dishes in the evening
- Clean kitchen surfaces
- Vacuum heavy traffic zones
- Water plants and check flowers

Which Room Are You In?

Kitchen
Select your task

Meeting and greeting your utensils
page 16

Posing with and using your equipment
page 18

Washing the dishes – by hand or machine
page 20

Being king of your kitchen
page 22

Cleaning the refrigerator
page 24

Cleaning your oven and microwave
page 26

Dealing with trash and recycling
page 28

Stocking your larder
page 30

Utility Room
Select your task

Getting to know your washing machine
page 42

Learning the laundry lingo
page 43

Washing your clothes the right way
page 44

How to handwash your clothes
page 46

Hanging out your washing
page 47

Learning how to iron
page 50

Living Area
Select your task

Tidying and de-junking
page 58

Dusting
page 60

Washing and wiping
page 62

Dealing with stains
page 64

Keeping home warm and safe
page 66

Looking after fabrics and furnishings
page 68

Flawless floors
page 70

Vacuuming
page 72

Dining Room
Select your task

Deciding seating plan
page 80

Laying the table
page 81

Decorating the table
page 82

Folding napkins
page 82

Flower arranging
page 83

Feeding guests
page 84

Watering guests
page 85

Carving a whole chicken
page 90

Home Office
Select your task

Making paper work for you
page 94

Prioritizing, filing and storing
page 95

Caring for houseplants in the office
page 96

Pets in the office and the home
page 98

Bedroom
Select your task

Taking care of beds
page 104

Making your bed
page 107

Sorting out your wardrobe
page 108

20 things a smart man should know
page 111

Dress sense
page 112

Domestic god in the bedroom
page 114

Guest who's coming to stay
page 118

Packing a good suitcase
page 120

Bathroom
Select your task

Top-to-toe hygiene
page 126

Cleaning your bathroom
page 128

Unblocking a toilet
page 130

Creating a home spa
page 132

Learning to relax
page 134

Stocking your first aid and medicine cupboard
page 136

Garage
Select your task

Basic car maintenance
page 150

Checking tyre pressure
page 152

Changing the oil
page 154

Washing your car
page 158

Cycle essentials
page 166

Cycle maintenance
page 168

Cycle tyre pressure
page 170

KITCHEN

Windows
Wash your windows regularly to improve the atmosphere and the light.

Plant Life
Herbs generally thrive on a sunny windowsill.

Keep it Clean
Sink and worktop hygiene is extremely important in the kitchen. Keep important, everyday equipment on the worktop and store the rest.

'A GOOD KITCHEN SHOULD BE SUFFICIENTLY REMOTE FROM THE PRINCIPAL APARTMENTS OF THE HOUSE, THAT THE MEMBERS, VISITORS, OR GUESTS OF THE FAMILY, MAY NOT PERCEIVE THE ODOUR INCIDENT TO COOKING, OR HEAR THE NOISE OF CULINARY OPERATIONS.'

Mrs. Isabella Beeton, Book of Household Management, 1861

The Oven

Wipe tiles and walls near the oven every day. Clean your oven more than once in a blue moon.

Cloth Cleaning

Clean your cloths and tea towels every couple of days.

Kitchen

I f you are always in the kitchen at parties, don't worry – you are in the right place. Kitchens are usually warm and welcoming places, the hub of domestic and social activity, the HQ of the household operation. It's often the first room people enter on getting up and returning home. We gather in the kitchen to chat, exchange news about our day, read the papers, open the post, eat informally and even relax. These are the positive, nurturing aspects of the kitchen. The downside, on the other hand, is that kitchens contain not only the strategic equipment needed in any headquarters but also its collateral debris. The kitchen is a magnet for clutter and needs regular attention, plus a few simple rules.

Bad news first – let's start with the no-nos, on the opposite page.

CHORE CHART: WHAT TO DO WHEN

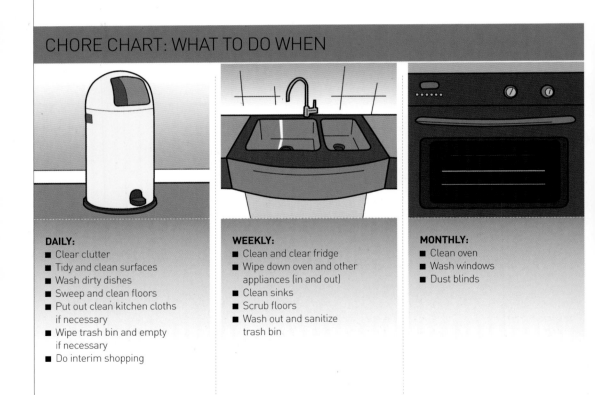

DAILY:
- Clear clutter
- Tidy and clean surfaces
- Wash dirty dishes
- Sweep and clean floors
- Put out clean kitchen cloths if necessary
- Wipe trash bin and empty if necessary
- Do interim shopping

WEEKLY:
- Clean and clear fridge
- Wipe down oven and other appliances (in and out)
- Clean sinks
- Scrub floors
- Wash out and sanitize trash bin

MONTHLY:
- Clean oven
- Wash windows
- Dust blinds

X NO-NOS

All the following activities could seriously damage your health:

1. ALL WASHED UP

In the context of the kitchen, 'all washed up' is a very positive condition and one to which you should aspire. Unwashed dishes are not only visually unappealing; but also provide a perfect home for organisms invisible to the naked eye. In those countries where cockroaches and other ugly, resourceful insects are regular, if unwanted, house guests, these are rather more macro than micro. Piles of dirty dishes and pans are nasty on all fronts, and what's more, you risk running out of clean crockery and glasses.

2. TRASH THE TRASH

Overflowing, unwashed trash bins are also high on the no-no list for many of the same reasons. They are unattractive, unsavoury, unhygienic – the list of 'uns' goes on and on. Take the trash out every evening and give the bin a quick wipe before putting a new bin liner inside. Once a week wash it out thoroughly. Keep a lid on your trash – you know it makes sense.

3. WIPE, WASH, DRY

What's the big deal? A cloth is a cloth is a cloth, isn't it? Wrong. Cloths have vocations. Dishcloths should be devoted to washing dishes and worktops; tea towels are dedicated to drying the dishes and floor cloths should only ever be used for mopping up spills and things on the floor. Towels were invented to dry your hands. You must be similarly single-minded in your role as kitchen carer – failing to wash cloths regularly is negligence of the highest domestic order. Dirty cloths are hazardous to your health and have to go.

4. SURFACE TENSION

After preparing a meal, wipe down all working surfaces, removing food, grease and other debris. Dirty worktops, ovens and sinks are health and safety hazards. What's more, they are unlikely to be the first thing you relish seeing in the morning, particularly if you are feeling rather delicate. The cat might enjoy that pool of sticky, smelly tuna oil in the sink, but you will not find its residual odour as tempting when it greets you the next day. It takes seconds to wipe down all the surfaces – it takes hours to remove the consequences of inaction.

Kitchen Utensils

S uch kitchen equipment these days is of such excellent design and made from such shiny metal that every self-respecting Domestic God will actually enjoy shopping for spatulas and the like. Even shed-owning guys will not be able to resist all the electrical attachments and smart tools that constitute the 21st century batterie de cuisine.

Not many males would be found without a bottle opener and a corkscrew on or about their person and you will no doubt own a tin opener from camping days, and even the odd pan. You may have begged, borrowed or inherited a kettle, toaster and teapot and your home will hopefully have a heating implement (whether microwave, stove, oven, Aga or barbecue).

DOMESTIC GOD IN THE KITCHEN

Domestic Gods in the kitchen will need all or almost all of the following (and your choice from those over the page) to complete their range:

- SMALL AND MEDIUM-SIZED NON-STICK FRYING PANS
- SELECTION OF SAUCEPANS OF DIFFERENT SIZES (STAINLESS STEEL OR CAST-IRON)
- ROASTING TINS (SMALL AND LARGE)
- WOK (ASK FOR ONE FOR YOUR NEXT BIRTHDAY)
- BAMBOO OR METAL STEAMER (FOR VEGETABLES)
- PLASTIC CHOPPING BOARDS (TWO OR THREE – FOR RAW, COOKED AND SMELLY FOOD)
- VEGETABLE PEELER
- GRATER
- JUICER
- 2 OR 3 WOODEN SPOONS

- MEASURING SPOONS AND JUG
- WEIGHING SCALES
- MIXING BOWLS (SMALL AND LARGE)
- SPATULA
- POTATO MASHER
- COLANDER
- SIEVE
- SELECTION OF KNIVES (ALL-PURPOSE, PARING, CARVING AND BREAD KNIFE) AND KNIFE SHARPENER
- STURDY KITCHEN SCISSORS
- LARGE FORK (FOR HELP WHEN CARVING)
- CLOTHS (FOR DISHES AND FLOORS),
- SPONGES, TEA TOWELS, METAL AND NYLON-MESH SCRUBBERS

- KITCHEN TOWEL (HYGIENIC AND HELPFUL – DON'T RUN OUT)
- OVEN MITT OR GLOVES
- BOTTLE BRUSH
- WASHING UP BOWL AND DRYING RACK

- STORAGE JARS, CONTAINERS, FREEZER BAGS AND TUBS
- COOKERY BOOKS
- SALT AND PEPPER SHAKERS

Time and motion

You'll need to store all of these items in cupboards and drawers that will require regular cleaning. If shelves are exposed, dirt and dust will gather quickly, so avoid open shelving if possible. Organize your equipment intelligently. Keep pans near the cooker – they can take the heat and you won't have to go on a walkabout to find them when needed. You can hang up pots and pans if space or design dictates, but make sure they are clean before use. Always have an oven glove at the ready near the heat of the action and make sure the equipment you need for cooking is close at hand too.

Plate it up

Naturally, you will need enough crockery and cutlery so as not to run out when some of it is in the dishwasher (not when it is piled up, unwashed, close to or in the sink) – and enough to entertain a number of friends. Build up your collection gradually, with the ultimate goal of a matching set for, say, six to eight people (plates, side plates, soup and dessert bowls etc.) plus cutlery. Check both are dishwasher-proof before purchase. Keep knives, forks and spoons in a divided drawer near the sink or dishwasher to save time when putting them away after drying. Give the drawer a regular clean. Try to store glasses and china within striking distance of the sink or dishwasher – time and motion are very important in the kitchen. Don't put cups and mugs in with glasses or you will break one or the other eventually.

At the sharp end

It may sound unlikely to the currently single, but you will probably form a deep attachment to your knife or knives once you have met your match. Spend the extra money to get a top quality sharp knife – it's really worth it. Clean it with hot water and a mild detergent and wipe immediately after. Don't put your kitchen knives in the dishwasher (more about dishwashers soon) or you risk damaging the blade. Store your knives in a special unit or use a magnetic bar; you may do serious damage to both blade and fingers if they are kept loose in a drawer. Never leave knives in the washing-up water. Value your fingertips and those of your partner or guests. To remove any lingering odours, rub with a slice of lemon, rinse and dry. This works for wooden worktops, too. To remove stubborn stains from a steel knife, dip in diluted lemon juice and rub vigorously with a steel wool pad. Sharpen your knives regularly.

USEFUL EXTRAS

- COOKING THERMOMETER
- BLENDER OR FOOD PROCESSOR (FOR THE CHRISTMAS LIST, OR YOUR MUM'S OLD MODEL)
- COFFEE GRINDER AND COFFEE MAKER (YOUR CHOICE)
- WHISK (HAND OR ELECTRIC)
- ROLLING PIN
- CAKE TIN (FOR ADVANCED COOKING AND REALLY SHOWING OFF)
- PAPER AND PENCILS FOR SHOPPING LISTS AND REMINDERS AND LABELS FOR FOOD
- PROTECTIVE APRON (FUNCTIONAL RATHER THAN FASHIONABLE)
- CHOPSTICKS
- FONDUE SET (USE TO MELT CHEESE, CHOCOLATE AND YOUR PARTNER'S HEART)
- WAFFLE MAKER
- RICE COOKER (FOR GREAT GRAINS EVERY TIME)
- PASTA MACHINE (FOR THE ADVANCED COOK)
- STAINLESS STEEL LADEL
- CHEESE SLICER
- OIL DRIZZLER
- GARLIC PRESS
- RAMEKINS (FOR SOUFFLÉS, CRÈMES BRÛLÉES AND PÂTÉS AND OTHER THINGS WITH ACCENTS)
- CHALK BOARD FOR REMINDERS AND HOUSEHOLD MESSAGES
- TIMER
- HOTPLATE OR TRIVET (FOR PROTECTING SURFACES FROM THE HOT STUFF)
- HEART-SHAPED METAL MOULD (FOR FRYING EGGS ON VALENTINE'S DAY)
- SHOPPING TROLLEY (SMART AND PRACTICAL – YOU'LL LEARN TO LIKE IT)
- MUSHROOM BRUSH

DOMESTIC GOD'S HOT TIP

Kettles generally boil more quickly than pans (even with lids on). Boil water for your pasta in a kettle rather than a pan for speed and convenience.

Kitchen Utensils: Use or Pose?

D o you want to impress in the kitchen? Now's your chance to find out how. Amateur chefs like you have the world at their fingertips when it comes to the range of kitchen utensils available today. However, take care – some items are more ostentatious than efficacious. You don't want to look like mutton dressed as lamb. Use this chart when purchasing key items. It's a sort of kitchen confidential, so keep it on a 'need to know' basis only.

USE OR POSE: A GUIDE TO THE STARS

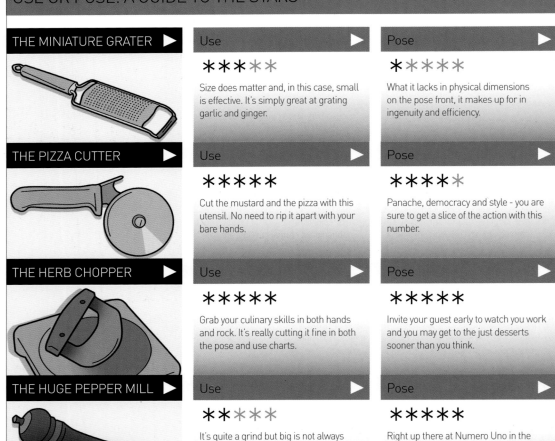

THE MINIATURE GRATER ▶

Use ▶
★★★✶✶
Size does matter and, in this case, small is effective. It's simply great at grating garlic and ginger.

Pose ▶
★✶✶✶✶
What it lacks in physical dimensions on the pose front, it makes up for in ingenuity and efficiency.

THE PIZZA CUTTER ▶

Use ▶
★★★★★
Cut the mustard and the pizza with this utensil. No need to rip it apart with your bare hands.

Pose ▶
★★★★✶
Panache, democracy and style - you are sure to get a slice of the action with this number.

THE HERB CHOPPER ▶

Use ▶
★★★★★
Grab your culinary skills in both hands and rock. It's really cutting it fine in both the pose and use charts.

Pose ▶
★★★★★
Invite your guest early to watch you work and you may get to the just desserts sooner than you think.

THE HUGE PEPPER MILL ▶

Use ▶
★★✶✶✶
It's quite a grind but big is not always best. Its size makes it better for brandishing than flavouring.

Pose ▶
★★★★★
Right up there at Numero Uno in the pose charts. Spice things up at the table in grand style.

CHINESE BAMBOO STEAMER ▶

Use ▶

★★★★✶

Stay healthy, save energy and enjoy stacks of goodness with this steamer. It's the ultimate in multi-tasking kitchen equipment.

Pose ▶

★★★★★

Watch out for heaps of steamy looks when you use this utensil. Aim as high as you want on the pose front.

PESTLE AND MORTAR ▶

Use ▶

★★★★✶

New Age meets Stone Age in this hands-on, practical piece of equipment. Herbs and spices – no better way to mix and grind.

Pose ▶

★★★★★

Traditional and trendy, this utensil takes you back to your loincloth. Add a dash of panache to the kitchen.

PASTA SERVER ▶

Use ▶

★★★★✶

Don't lose your noodles or let slip your spaghetti. Keep slippery strands under control when serving at dinner parties.

Pose ▶

★★✶✶✶

Clever and stylish. Deliver with oodles of style and no dry-cleaning bills when serving your beloved.

PASTA MEASURER ▶

Use ▶

★★★★✶

No more cooking enough spaghetti for six when you're planning a romantic dinner à deux. A kitchen calculator.

Pose ▶

★★★★★

Get a grip on dimensions and portions with this piece of equipment. It doesn't just add up, it measures style.

Whose Turn to Wash the Dishes?

Pans with really stubborn food residues can be left to soak overnight, or you can fill them with water, add detergent and allow the leftovers to simmer on the heat. The food will loosen gradually and you can then wash up as normal. To clean a scorched pan, fill with water, add a few tablespoons of bicarbonate of soda and boil until the scorched parts come loose. Don't leave the room during this process.

Stacks of time

Treat the job of stacking dirty dishes near the sink as if it were an exercise in logic, time and motion. Organization and preparation save time and muscles later. The order for washing things is least dirty first, so try to prepare them in that order, keeping like-items together. To wash a delicate glass alongside a huge pan is a no-no. Before you embark on your mission, scrape off food and heavy soiling using a wooden spoon or spatula and place debris in a handy container (unless you have a waste disposal unit). Pour fat and oil into the container rather than down the drain. Dispose of contents carefully in the trash.

That sinking feeling

There's no denying that washing the dishes is up there with ironing on the list of least popular household activities. However, in the interests of hygiene it is a must. You can't eat from paper plates or pizza boxes forever. Whether you are a two-legged dishwasher or lucky enough to own an automatic one, it is important to understand the basic principles of sink hygiene. Some people actually relish washing up at the end of the day; it's a form of therapy, an opportunity to wind down, commune and communicate with one's partner over the washing, drying and tidying process.

Soak and destroy

Try to reserve the kitchen sink for food-related activities only, as other household mess can bring about germ transfer. Don't risk cross-contamination with cloths – use dishcloths for washing dishes and tea towels for drying them. Don't even think about using a floor cloth for either mission. It's a good idea to clean up your pots, pans, bowls and work surfaces as you go. Paper towels are good for mopping up spills and don't spread germs, since they are disposable.

Don't forget – we are never alone. Pests love dirty dishes that, if left for any length of time, become smelly. Soon bacteria multiply then invite their friends round for a leftovers party. Worse still, ants and cockroaches may gate crash. If you can't wash-up last minute items before serving food, fill them with hot water (plus detergent if they're greasy) and allow to soak until after the meal.

Drain and dry

Place items properly in the drying rack so that the water can drain off. Horizontal is not helpful. If you leave things to dry on their own, or to air dry, as it is called in all the best kitchens, put them away as soon as they're dry. Leaving them overnight is not a good idea, as they will be dirty again by the time you put them in the cupboard. If you dry with a tea towel, make sure it is a clean, fresh one. Go easy with glasses. Wrap the towel around your forefinger and middle finger, insert into the glass and gently rub the inner surface. Try to remove spots and streaks from all items.

Finale

Make sure your bowl, sink and surrounding surfaces are clean once you have finished. Replace your dishcloth and tea towels regularly with clean ones. This is a germ-intensive area and should be kept sparkling. Now doesn't that feel better? If the sink is blocked, pour a small cup of bicarbonate of soda down, followed by the same amount of vinegar. Allow it to fizz for ten minutes and then pour boiling water slowly down the sink. It's like a hangover cure – things are clearer afterwards.

DOMESTIC GOD'S HOT TIP

Just 30 minutes of moderately vigorous activity at the sink burns off about 80 calories. If all goes well, more calories could be worked off a Domestic God later.

HOT AND BUBBLY

Fill your bowl	Lovely bubbly	Flex the pecs	Rinsing is right

Fill your bowl or sink with hot water (not right to the top) and add detergent – check the instructions and don't go overboard. If you put on protective plastic gloves, you'll be able to use really hot water, which is more hygienic and cleans more deeply; cool is not cool for dirt and debris.

Now it's time to sink your hands into those lovely clean bubbles. Wash the glasses first, one by one if they are your best wine or champagne glasses given to you by a beloved aunt. Cutlery comes next, then china, followed by large bowls and dishes. Pots and pans dive in last. You may need to change the water in between if it gets very dirty or if all the suds vanish.

Wash the dishes with a cloth, sponge or brush and flex your biceps slightly but not excessively. A circular motion works well. If you have to use an abrasive scourer for stubborn stains, use the appropriate one for the surface or you will damage it. Be very gentle with non-stick pans; treat them like your partner – with respect and care.

Rinse all items in hot, clean water. This follow-up action has a number of advantages – hygienic (it destroys more germs), aesthetic (it prevents streaking) and strategic (it accelerates the drying process). And when you next have a glass of champagne, it means only the right bubbles will fizz and float to the surface. Rinsing is right, so go for it.

DOMESTIC GOD'S BEST FRIEND

Don't let pets walk on worktops and tables – either while preparing food or at any other time. Little feet spread diseases, just like all our coughs and sneezes.

X NO-NOS

As with most household activities, note some no-nos. Always check the instructions on any equipment before you put it in the dishwasher. The following don't fare well in the machine:

- DELICATE CHINA OR CERAMIC ITEMS
- OLD GLASS, LEAD CRYSTAL AND FRAGILE GLASS
- HAND-PAINTED, GILDED OR SILVERED CHINA OR GLASSWARE
- ANYTHING WITH A BONE, BAMBOO, IVORY OR WOODEN HANDLE
- YOUR BELOVED KITCHEN KNIVES

- THIN PLASTIC BOWLS AND CUPS (THEY WILL CHANGE SHAPE!)
- SILVERWARE – IF YOU DO PUT IN SILVERWARE, DON'T WASH IT TOGETHER WITH STAINLESS STEEL OR IT MAY BECOME STAINED
- WOODEN SALAD BOWLS

Dishwasher magic

Dishwashers are wonderful things (the mechanical ones have a certain edge over the two-legged equivalent). Once you have one at your disposal, you will wonder how you ever managed without it.

Loaded

Loading dishwashers demands a methodical, even scientific approach. Gaps are required to help circulate the water – overloading is a no-no. It might help to think of the dishwasher as a 360-degree shower cabinet in which you are to enjoy a top-to-toe cleanse. Remove obvious debris before entry (like taking your clothes off) and even indulge in a quick pre-treatment rinse (like you would do in a spa). You don't want bits flying around and damaging delicate parts, do you? Assume a position in unrestricted firing line of the water spray. Turn your dirty surfaces towards the water, arranging various bits appropriately (spoons and forks should be alternately upright and upside down and tall, bulky items must not block the spray).

Some dishwashers require you to load from the back forwards thereby making good use of all the space. In those machines not equipped with sensors, the top level is the place for glasses and fragile items (cups, mugs, small bowls etc.) and things that should not get too hot – think of it as the 'above the neck' zone. You wouldn't want really hot water in your eyes or up your nose, would you? Don't let glasses make contact – they may break or chip. Remember, this is the 'delicates' deck. The more robust lower area is for plates, dishes and pans.

Kitchen King or Kitchen Slave?

Are you in charge of the kitchen or is it in charge of you? Establish a routine and you will soon reign in your domain. Books on the shelves, food in the refrigerator or in the cupboard, pans where they belong, cutlery in the drawer, crockery safely stored, shoes and clothes in the hall or bedroom, briefcases, satchels and rucksacks in the office, partner in the garage – everything in its place. That way you will always end up with less clutter, fewer germs and minimal accidents.

Clear and clean the surfaces, making sure the sink, worktops, table and cooker are wiped down after use and at regular intervals in between meals. Clean them thoroughly with hot, soapy water and sanitize kitchen worktops with a disinfectant kitchen cleaner. Where food, spills and grease lurk, there you'll find microbes. Wash dishes as soon as possible (see page 20), use chopping boards rather than a worktop for preparing ingredients and make sure you sanitize them afterwards.

Are you for the chop?

Take great care to avoid contact between cooked or ready-to-eat foods and raw food, both in storage and preparation. Don't use the same knife or chopping board for raw meat and cooked foods, unless you thoroughly sanitize it afterwards. The best solution is to have two boards (plastic is best) and even a third, smaller one on which to chop smelly food such as garlic, chillies and onions. It may sound rather over the top, but it is important. If you go for wood, keep it clean by rubbing it regularly with a mixture of lemon juice and salt. Sanitize your worktop after preparing raw meat on it. A weekly scald with boiling water is an effective way of sterilizing your board.

Keep your food cupboards clean, cool, tidy and dry. Always wash your hands before preparing or touching food. If you have been stroking pets or handling leftovers, dirty washing, soil or trash, wash your hands in hot water and soap for several seconds. You don't need to be reminded that this applies to most personal activities. Buy some pleasant-smelling, moisturizing, antibacterial handwash for the kitchen and utility room (OK, it's

not as much fun as a CD but it's better than listening to the sound of Salmonella, Staphylococcus and the E. Coli band).

Don't be floored

Use paper towels to mop up small spills and messages from pets. Try to keep a permanent stock of regular or recycled kitchen towel – it is a lifesaver, and a quick and hygienic way of dealing with unsavoury spillages. Remember to sweep the floor regularly – crumbs, debris and all kinds of nastiness set up camp there. Give your floor a proper clean at least once a fortnight. Floor wipes are a handy way of keeping certain floor surfaces clean without too much effort if the traditional mop and bucket of hot, soapy water technique doesn't appeal.

The good news is that polishing is generally not a good idea unless you want to slip, glide and slide effortlessly but dangerously between appliances. If you have a stone floor, sweep and vacuum regularly and give it a weekly (OK, fortnightly) wash with soapy water followed by a rinse and dry. Alternatively, you could use a proprietary floor cleaner. Ditto for glazed tiled floors. Sweep sealed wooden floors and wash occasionally with a damp cloth or sponge – a wax improves the shine. Vinyl and linoleum floors can be mopped clean. If you are the proud owner of a stone or tiled floor, remember that they are not known for their bouncy properties. If you drop anything, it will break nine out of ten times.

QUESTIONS AND ANSWERS

I DON'T KNOW THE DIFFERENCE BETWEEN A DETERGENT, A DISINFECTANT AND AN ANTIBACTERIAL CLEANER? DO I REALLY HAVE TO WASTE TIME READING THE INSTRUCTIONS?

Detergents such as washing-up liquids, dissolve grease, oil and dirt. Disinfectants, such as bleach, are designed to kill germs. Use with care – they are powerful agents. Anti-bacterial cleaners kill germs too and can come in spray form. They are a type of disinfectant. Yes, always read the instructions carefully.

WHAT'S THE BIG DEAL ABOUT TAKING OUT THE TRASH EVERY EVENING?

Germs love trash, and unless you have a passion for germs, empty the trash regularly, particularly in the summer. Use a bin with a lid and always use a liner. Tie the bag before removal or you will spill debris onto the floor. Clean the bin out with hot water and disinfectant regularly. That's the deal – not so big, is it?

If you limit the size of the bin, it will be emptied more frequently (by you) and therefore be less prone to unpleasant odours.

WHAT'S ALL THIS NONSENSE ABOUT DISINFECTING DISHCLOTHS?

Nonsense it isn't. Kitchen sponges, dishcloths and tea towels are often contaminated with bacteria, even though they look reasonably clean. Launder them frequently on the hot cycle of your washing machine. Then dry them thoroughly. If left moist bacteria can sneak back into the fabric. Paper towels are a hygienic alternative although expensive.

WHAT DO I DO ABOUT INSECTS IN THE KITCHEN?

Try not to use aerosol sprays in the kitchen. Hang up an insecticidal strip to control flies and wasps. Trace the ant run back to the entry spot and put down ant poison. Put a bay leaf on shelves to deter cockroaches. They love dank, dark, dirty spots. If you have an infestation of ants or cockroaches, call in the experts.

DISHWASHER SAFE?

Try to get to know your dishwasher, its likes and dislikes, what makes it tick and keeps it ticking. Read the instructions carefully and keep them in a safe place. Your relationship needs maintaining, just like the machine – check how to replenish the salt, keep its surfaces and filter clean and always use the right detergent. If it dumps you without warning, you will be at a loss. From time to time use vinegar rather than dishwasher powder to give your machine and its mechanics a thorough clean on the inside and a shiny finish.

- READ THE MANUAL AND FILE IT SOMEWHERE SAFE.
- CHECK THE FILTER REGULARLY AND REMOVE ANYTHING BLOCKING IT.
- CHECK THE SALT AND KEEP ALL SURFACES CLEAN.
- ALWAYS USE THE RIGHT DETERGENT – NO SUBSTITUTES.
- THE HIGHEST TEMPERATURE CYCLE COMBATS THE MOST GERMS.
- USE ECONOMY CYCLE WHENEVER POSSIBLE.
- WHEN WASHING GLASSWARE ONLY, RUN THE DISHWASHER WITHOUT DETERGENT FROM TIME TO TIME.
- ALWAYS PLACE SHARP KNIVES BLADE DOWNWARDS.
- UNLOAD YOUR MACHINE AS SOON AS CYCLE HAS FINISHED.

- DON'T GO ON VACATION WITH AN UNWASHED LOAD IN THE DISHWASHER.
- KEEP THE DOOR SHUT OR PETS WILL CLIMB INSIDE.
- DON'T WASH THINGS IN THE DISHWASHER THAT AREN'T INTENDED FOR SUCH A FATE (I.E. CLOTHS, SHOES, PETS).

Refrigerators and Freezers

When did you last see your refrigerator naked with the lights on? Has it been a while? If so, it's time to change things. Once a season at least, strip your refrigerator bare and give it a thorough going over, unplugging it before you embark on the mission.

A cool clean refrigerator can help you get the most freshness, taste and nutrition from its contents. You may think that cold equals clean, but although the temperature may be very low, some bacteria manage to survive and create food safety problems. Remove the shelves and wash both sides thoroughly with hot, soapy water. Start at the top of the refrigerator to avoid having to start all over again. Get rid of all the spills, mould and mildew. You can use a paste of bicarbonate of soda and water (4 tbsp of each) to clean the inside. This will also help eliminate stale smells. A dish of charcoal left overnight helps to remove any obstinate odours. Rinse with a damp cloth, dry with a clean one. Clean the door (inside and out), the seals and the handle. Take the opportunity to evict squatters – food well past its eat-by date, shrivelled leftovers, anything sporting unfashionable mould and items that were in there untouched last time you cleaned the refrigerator. Don't forget to put the plug back in the socket!

I'm too cool for my kitchen
Today, refrigerators can keep track of their own contents, connect to your computer and place orders directly online without you stirring from your bed. Some come equipped with televisions, cameras, water dispensers, ice makers, and facilities for dishing out recipes, nutritional information and emails. The only downside is, they can't self-clean. Your role is to invent one that can, or do the job yourself. Think of the refrigerator as your inbox of emails – old messages are stale or potentially damaging. They overflow, get blocked and can contaminate. Sensible, safe storage – that's the most obvious answer.

UFOs
Don't overload your freezer. Identify each item with a label showing contents and date of entry (not necessary for packaged, labelled foods). UFOs (unidentifiable frozen objects) should be treated without mercy. You don't know how long they have been in there or even what they contain. Freeze in small quantities rather than large ones for speed and safety. Never refreeze foods once they have thawed out. After purchase, take frozen food home quickly and put straight in the freezer (unless you are going to eat it that day, in which case put it in the refrigerator). Don't leave it in your rucksack or briefcase or under the desk at work. Put a cool bag or cool box on your birthday wish list.

Keep fresh or frozen meat, fish and poultry in its original wrapping. You might want to put food in a plastic bag if you plan to keep it in the freezer for more than two months. Make sure food is stored in containers that are both air- and moisture-proof. The temperature should be minus 18 degrees celsius or below. Allow meat, poultry and fish to defrost slowly in the refrigerator or defrost in a microwave. Once thawed, refrigerate for up to 24 hours or cook immediately. You can then refreeze.

Keep it on ice
Coffee kept in the freezer stays fresh longer. Always have some in stock for unplanned lazy mornings spent with your beloved. Freeze some croissants and bagels to go with it. Keep some bacon or smoked salmon on ice, too, if they take your fancy, but not eggs. Should you find yourself in possession of leftover white and red wine, pour it into an ice tray and you will always have small amounts on hand for sauces.

Put a mint leaf or a raspberry in each compartment of the ice tray before filling with water. Drop nonchalantly into a cocktail glass to impress at parties.

Keep frozen herbs and garlic for soups, casseroles and emergencies. Try to store the basics for a 'cook from frozen' meal for two, four or six people (depending on how popular you are) for short-notice entertaining or one of those unplanned late-night invitations of the 'everybody come back to my place for something to eat' kind.

Keep it clean
You will need to clean the freezer from time to time. Unplug the refrigerator and wipe up crumbs and spills. You can empty all the shelves or just move food from one side to the other as you go. It's a great opportunity to remove UFOs and things beyond human consumption. If you want to defrost a manual-defrost freezer compartment, unplug the refrigerator, take out the contents, put in a cool box if you have one and then place a pan of hot water in the freezer. The ice should become soft enough to remove with your hands (but don't use spiky metal objects for the job). Empty the tray, clean the freezer and you are back in business. Oh yes, plug it back in now, too.

GOOD REFRIGERATOR/BAD REFRIGERATOR

Open your refrigerator and compare its contents to a work of art. A minimalist, two-tone canvas by an artist working in cardboard and aluminium? Or a luscious portrayal of nature's produce interspersed with the best of 21st-century manmade products? Ask yourself if you could make an impromptu meal with its contents (not using the phone number for pizza delivery)? If you were feeling unwell and unable to go out for a few days, could you survive happily on what you have stored in the refrigerator? Just how many vitamins could you identify and enjoy munching on the food inside? If the answers are no, not really and none, you will know which category (and takeout trap) you fall into.

Before ▶   After ▶

COOL FACTS

DON'T OVERLOAD

Don't overload the refrigerator. Proper air circulation equals proper refrigeration. And you will be able to find things more easily. Put the new container of milk behind the one already in the refrigerator to avoid cheesy milk lurking at the back.

Don't keep opening the door – it increases both the temperature and your waist measurement.

TEMPERATURE

The temperature in the door will fluctuate most due to frequent opening. Use it for pickles, salad dressings, condiments, soft drinks, beer and wine rather than milk and eggs and products most sensitive to temperature changes.

Give your refrigerator a spring clean every season but a good wipe every week and when you put your new shopping in.

THERMOMETER

Invest in a refrigerator thermometer (they cost less than a beer) to alert you to any temperature problems. Put it in the middle of the unit and check every week. The temperature should be at least four degrees celsius or lower.

Heat rises (remember your school days?) so the coolest part is likely to be at the bottom of the unit or at the back of the shelf. Keep meats, fish, poultry and milk here.

SPECIAL COMPARTMENTS

If your model has special compartments for cheese, meats, fruit and vegetables use them for the products for which they are designed, except for the egg holder. Throw this away or use it as a mould for homemade candles or a foot spa for a pet tarantula. Keep eggs on the main shelf in the shop carton – that is where they belong. Use them within four weeks of purchase.

Cover food before refrigerating and store raw foods below cooked foods. Promptly cool any leftovers and use within two or three days.

Ovens, Hobs and Microwaves: Taking the Heat in the Kitchen

C ome on guys, the oven may not be a page-turner of a subject, but there is some good news to keep you going – three little words in fact (or four without a hyphen) – they are The Self-Cleaning Oven. What could be simpler? All you have to do is read the manual and get out of the kitchen when things get a bit hot. For other appliances and surfaces, you may need a bit more effort though.

Microwave magic

Although they cook as if by magic, microwave ovens require a magician's assistant to keep them clean and in full working order. Food often makes a mess when cooked in a microwave. Check the manufacturer's instructions first for recommended methods and cleaning products but a quick twice weekly wipe with warm water and a mild detergent should suffice. Don't use a commercial oven cleaner or the magic tricks may go horribly wrong.

Remove the circular plate and wash in the sink, removing all food deposits. Wash the top and bottom of the microwave, its sides, door (inside and out) and seals. Wipe it dry. Be extra careful with the control panel and don't use scourers. Some people swear by putting a wet dishcloth in the centre of the microwave and turning the machine on high for 30-40 seconds. The steam will loosen spills and you can use the heated cloth to wipe the inside clean. Careful, it's hot!

MICROWAVE MOMENTS

1. Read instructions on packaging before cooking.

2. Defrost food in the microwave only if you plan to use immediately.

3. Cut food into evenly sized pieces to microwave or place larger items on the outer edge of the dish.

4. Rotate and stir foods to ensure even cooking. Cover food to avoid spattering.

5. If reheating food, ensure it is very hot.

6. Always check the tray, container or utensil is microwave-friendly.

7. Deodorize by placing a bowl of water inside containing four slices of fresh lemon, or two tablespoons of lemon juice.

8. Cook on high for 30-60 seconds.

DIRTY TRAPS

Can openers with cutting wheels
Food can lodge between the wheels and then contaminate the next product it opens. Give it a good rub with a toothbrush dipped in hot water and detergent or put it in the dishwasher (check it is dishwasher-proof first).

Wooden spoons with splits and spiky surfaces
Germs lurk in the cracks. Dump them or make clothes for them.

HOT AND SOAPY: MANUAL CLEANING TECHNIQUES

If you have to 'switch to manual' for cleaning purposes, try to keep your hob and oven top clean all the time. Mop up spills immediately rather than waiting for them to form solid abstract art forms or lunar landscapes. Remove stubborn stains by covering them with hot, soapy water and then gently rubbing. Beware of using abrasive cleaning products and steel wool on certain surfaces and always check what the manufacturer's advise.

KEEP A COOL HEAD

Keep a cool head in the kitchen and wait for heating elements to chill before wiping them with a damp cloth soaked in mild detergent – singed cloth with burnt fingers is not a dish found much on the best menus. Removable parts of the oven can be put in hot, soapy water to clean. If you are a messy but forgetful cook, fear not – there will be more than enough reminders of the food you prepared on the walls and the worktops around the hob. Keep this space clean, too. It's not a contemporary art canvas but a work area.

WASH REGULARLY

Make sure you wash the grill pan regularly – don't let fat and other residues build up and form an unsightly mess to greet you or your romantically-inclined partner on a lazy Sunday morning. If you don't deal with it immediately after use, the fat will melt and splatter, then something unsavoury may hit the fan next time. More mess equals more work. It's not the nicest job, but it earns you lots of points. Place aluminium foil under the grill to catch the fat – this saves time scraping, soaking and washing the pan later.

PREVENTATIVE MEASURES

In fact, there are several preventative measures that can be taken on the oven-cleaning front. Instead of cooking food on the highest temperature setting and getting the contents of the pans over-excited, turn the heat down. Boiling the heck out of food is not good for the hob or for you. It eradicates taste, goodness and power. Gently does it, guys. Cooking is both a science and an art. It's therapy as well as thermal theory.

OVENLY BLISS

When tackling an oven not blessed with self-cleaning properties, prepare the ground first by placing newspaper on the floor beneath to catch any drips. Purchase a commercial cleaner suitable for your model and spray over the oven, protecting your hands and eyes as a safety measure. It's strong stuff, so don't clean the oven in just your underwear and remember to open a window.

The oven cleaner will spend a few hours taking effect (remember to close the oven door firmly), then you can wipe it off, along with the grease and grime, using kitchen towel or an old cloth that you are happy to throw out. Rinse the inside with a cloth soaked in plain water. Alternatively, rub the interior with wet wire wool before sprinkling with bicarbonate of soda (that old favourite). Rub clean with a damp cloth.

Treasure, Trash, Recycle: Save the World

C ast a glance around your kitchen and check for any appliances covered in dust, hidden unused in cupboards or still packed in the boxes in which they were purchased on impulse, or received unsolicited. How many times have you used that self-rotating yoghurt maker with built-in pancake thrower? Have you and your partner got more kettles and toasters than the local hotel?

If your kitchen equipment has not been used for six to nine months, take action. Only keep appliances you use frequently on the work surface – store less frequently used ones in a cupboard. Any more that you don't use, yet can't throw away because your partner's mother gave them to you, consign to the attic and bring them out when you have to. If any equipment dates back two centuries, check out how much it is worth before doing so!

Households in the developed world are incredibly efficient at generating vast mountains of trash every year. Some of it is non-biodegradable, but about two thirds is recyclable. Different countries and different government departments within them have specific laws and facilities; some are much more geared up for recycling than others. Research the what, where and how of recycling in your area and make an effort. It's not a big task. It's a small way of helping the world and those that come after you. You can help by buying recycled products in the first place of course – stationery, toilet paper, bottles, jars and boxes among them.

Set up a system that allows you to recycle paper, plastic, glass and metal objects. Storage solutions include colour-coded plastic boxes, recycled wooden crates (paint them if you're feeling particularly creative) and baskets. Use them to store items for recycling and for transporting them, if necessary, to the nearest recycling centre.

Find a convenient and safe place in the kitchen in which to store the boxes. If they are near the point of original use, you are more likely to sustain your good intentions, so see if they will fit under a kitchen unit or on shelves in the utility area. Stack the containers to save ground space if you need to and label them if they are all the same colour. Recycling is a good idea, so don't put it straight into the 'too hard' pile.

Let's focus on the obvious items:

RECYCLABLES

1. NEWSPAPER

Save your old newspapers, stationery, a assorted used paper sundries and store in a recyclable paper bag, a purpose-made wire rack or plastic crate. Allocate a place to keep it all together and delive or arrange for collection regularly. Don't create your own home-grown paper mountain, however biodegradable or well-intentioned. If your paper is not recyclable, donate it to a school or chari Take magazines to the local doctor's surgery and computer paper to schools. Re-house, recycle, remember.

2. PLASTIC

Most recyclable plastic features a C symbol on the base. Check for this whe purchasing and recycling. Store clean, plastic items (with lids removed) in a designated place. Reuse your plastic shopping bags rather than accumulatin a huge, unused pile. Shopping bags can be used as bin liners, laundry bags and shoe bags (for suitcases). Keep a couple in the car too, for gathering up litter.

3. GLASS

You generally need to recycle glass according to colour: clear, green or brow Sorting glass before you store it makes easier to deliver or have collected. Rinse out bottles, discard the corks but leave the labels on. If the bottle is particularly attractive, use it to serve water at your next dinner party. Pop in a slice of fresh lemon and a sprig of mint, and serve chilled water from the bottle.

4. ALUMINIMUM AND STEEL

OK, this is only slightly more demanding. Check human and pet food cans for a recycling symbol before rinsing them out. Foil packaging and takeout food trays may also be recycled but often have to be kept separately from tin cans, so check with your local government office. These materials can be magically transformed into new cans and car parts.

5. COMPOST

Keep fruit and vegetable peelings, teabags, coffee grounds, wood ash, shredded paper and cardboard for the compost. If you don't have an outdoor space, find an organization or individual who can use this household waste productively.

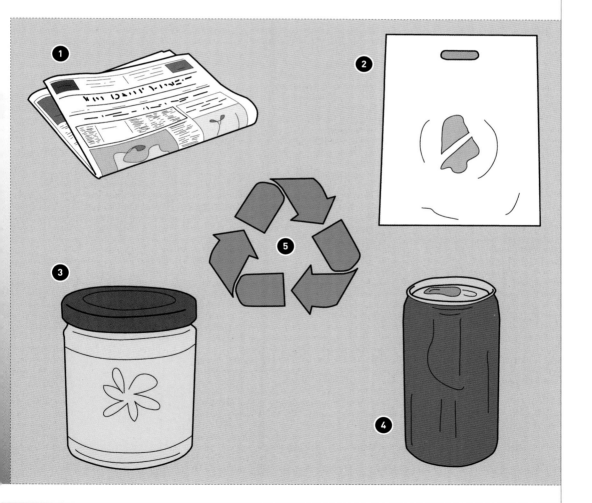

What's in Store?

Waintaining a well-stocked larder is a vital strategy for men in complete or even partial charge of the kitchen. Just think, our cavemen ancestors benefited from having the largest organic open-air market known to man right outside their dwellings (OK, so they did have to hunt and gather for the privilege). Nowadays the club and spear have been replaced by the somewhat less macho but often more reliable shopping trolley and credit card. Some guys still forage in the sea for food at the weekend, but there is almost always a back-up plan in case the fish want to be spared the rod.

LARDER PERFECTION

Let's identify the canned foods that you should try to keep in stock in the larder so you can cook a meal without needing to get extra supplies:

MUST HAVES

- FISH (TUNA, SARDINES, SALMON, CRAB)
- VEGETABLES (TOMATOES, SWEET CORN, ASPARAGUS, BEANS, PEAS, CHICK PEAS)
- FRUIT (PEACHES, APPLES, PEARS, RASPBERRIES ETC.)
- SOUP (THE USUAL SUSPECTS – TOMATO, CHICKEN, CLAM CHOWDER, PUMPKIN – PLUS LOBSTER BISQUE FOR A SPECIAL OCCASION)
- CUSTARD, RICE PUDDING (GREAT COMFORT FOOD)

ADD THESE

- STOCK CUBES (FOR SAUCES AND GRAVY)
- OLIVE OIL (FOR DRESSINGS)
- SUNFLOWER OIL (FOR STIR FRIES)
- VINEGAR (BALSAMIC, RED AND WHITE WINE, AND CHEAP VINEGAR FOR WASHING WINDOWS!)

- MUSTARD, PICKLES AND OTHER CONDIMENTS
- SALT AND PEPPER
- HERBS, SPICES AND CURRY POWDER
- TOMATO KETCHUP, PASTE, PURÉE AND SAUCES
- SOY SAUCE, TERIYAKI SAUCE, FISH SAUCE, COCONUT MILK (FOR ASIAN DISHES)
- TABASCO SAUCE, WORCESTERSHIRE SAUCE
- PESTO SAUCE (FOR PASTA)
- HONEY
- PEANUT BUTTER
- JAMS, MARMALADE AND JELLIES
- CHOCOLATE (TO MELT OVER ICE CREAM)
- COFFEE, TEA AND COCOA
- SHERRY, MADEIRA AND MARSALA (FOR SAUCES)

STAPLES

- PASTA, RICE, NOODLES (DON'T EVER RUN OUT!)

Being a 21st-century hunter-gatherer is frankly a much easier business. Nowadays, it's called shopping or marketing, and although it may not be your favourite activity, smartly stocked cupboards will really help you cook up a storm for your beloved at the drop of a hat or a loincloth. Call it cupboard love. The way to your partner's heart may be through the larder. And if you have a computer, you don't even have to leave home to reach target. Remember though, that a leisurely spot of shopping at the supermarket does burn up around 250 calories.

- COUSCOUS (FOR MORE ADVENTUROUS CUISINE)
- DRIED BEANS, LENTILS AND OTHER PULSES
- FLOUR
- BICARBONATE OF SODA (FOR STAINS AND ODOURS!)
- BAKING POWDER
- BREAKFAST CEREALS (HEALTHY AND LOW IN SUGAR)
- DRIED FRUIT (FOR OFFICE SNACKS AND BAKING)
- OLIVES (FOR COCKTAILS AND PASTA SAUCES)
- CRISPS, CRACKERS AND PRETZELS (FOR GUESTS)
- CHEESE BISCUITS (FOR DINNER PARTIES)
- SUGAR (BROWN AND WHITE)
- CONDENSED OR LONG-LIFE MILK (FOR EMERGENCIES AND SOME DESSERTS)

ADVENTUROUS STAPLES

- POLENTA
- JAPANESE UDON, SOBA AND RAMEN NOODLES
- REFRIED BEANS
- BAMBOO SHOOTS

- JAR OF ROASTED RED PEPPERS

HAVE TO HAND

- POTATOES – STORE IN A COOL, DARK PLACE
- ONIONS (RED AND WHITE) AND GARLIC – DON'T STORE IN REFRIGERATOR – INVEST IN A WIRE BASKET
- TOMATOES – KEEP IN A BOWL ON THE KITCHEN COUNTER
- LEMONS AND LIMES (FOR COCKTAILS)

KEEP IT COOL
MAKE SURE YOU HAVE SOME OR ALL OF THE FOLLOWING IN THE REFRIGERATOR (CHECKING DATES REGULARLY FOR FRESHNESS):

- BUTTER, MARGARINE, OLIVE OIL SPREAD
- MILK
- YOGHURT
- CHEESES (INC. PARMESAN)
- MEAT, FISH AND POULTRY (ON THE BOTTOM SHELF IF RAW)
- EGGS
- SALAD INGREDIENTS

- ROOT VEGETABLES (IN VEGETABLE DRAWER)
- FAVOURITE FRUIT (NOT BANANAS OR UNRIPENED FRUIT)
- FRESH PASTA
- READY-MADE SAUCES (FOR MEAT, FISH AND PASTA)
- MAYONNAISE

FROZEN MOMENTS
SMART FREEZING MEANS KEEPING SUPPLIES OF THE FOLLOWING ON ICE:

- MEAT (MINCED BEEF, SAUSAGES, BACON, BURGERS) AND POULTRY (CHICKEN – WHOLE, THIGHS, WINGS OR BREAST), FISH
- SELECTION OF FRUIT AND VEGETABLES
- ICE CREAM (VANILLA PLUS LUXURY FLAVOURS)
- FRESH PASTA
- BREAD, CROISSANTS, PIZZA BASES
- FRESH GINGER (FOR STIR-FRYING)
- EXTRA MILK
- BUTTER (SALTED AND UNSALTED)

STORING TIPS

Keep your larder and cupboard shelves clean, organizing the contents so that you can easily find a required item and recognize when you have run out.

Establish rows or collections of canned food, sauces, pasta and rice etc.

Rotate the cans, eat the oldest items first and evict any bulging or rusting cans.

Always read food labels to check sell-by dates plus storage and consumption information. Once opened, bottles or jars of food should usually be placed in the refrigerator (read the labels carefully).

Keep root vegetables away from other fruit and vegetables in a dark place.

Wash fruit and vegetables before eating and peel fruit and root vegetables.

After opening dried food (flour, rice, breakfast cereal) ensure that you reseal the container tightly or transfer to a storage jar to keep pests out.

Never put cans back in the refrigerator.

Transfer cooked food into a container or covered bowl and eat within two days.

Refrigerate fresh food as soon as possible after purchase (except for fruit in need of ripening and gourmet cheeses).

Store pet foods away from human food.

Before putting pre-packed foods in the deep freeze, check if they are suitable for freezing.

Food Facts

Imagine your body is an expensive, finely tuned sports car – you obviously want it to run on the best fuel available, right? The food pyramid below shows all the main food groups: you should eat more of the power foods at the base and less of those at the top. You know it makes sense!

IT'S ALL IN THE BALANCE

A balanced diet is important for long-term health and includes a combination of several different food types: grains and pulses; fresh fruit and vegetables; meat, fish and dairy products; fats, oils and sweets. The right balance allows you to maintain a healthy weight and get essential nutrients, such as fatty acids, proteins for repair and regeneration, and vitamins and minerals. A proper diet helps look after your heart and arteries, boost immunity and reduce the risk of certain cancers.

Go very easy on the foods at the top of the pyramid (right). Enjoy moderate amounts of the protein-rich foods and dairy items and minimize their fat content by trimming fat off meat and resisting chicken skin. The way food is prepared is also a factor – go for grilling rather than frying, unless it's a low-fat stir fry. Dump the breadcrumbs, batter, pastry and stuffing. Naked is good. The best cooking methods are steaming for vegetables, roasting and baking for meat and poaching for fish and eggs.

In general, men can get enough protein from their diets to allow them to eat less fatty and protein-rich food and more fruit, vegetables an carbohydrates. Munch away to your heart's content on fruit and vegetables guys. Otherwise this might be you:

ANYBODY OUT THERE?

Unfit man with beer belly seeks attractive partner with perfect physique. Must like fatty, processed foods, takeouts and sweet things. Lovers of romantic walks and home cooking need not apply.

FIVE ALIVE

Don't be a banana, eat one. You should consume at least five portions of fruit and vegetables a day. They are an excellent source of vitamins, minerals and fibre – and free of cholesterol. If you get a snack attack, eat an apple or a handful of dried fruit or nuts. When the object of your heart's desire in the office offers you a sweet but fattening temptation, whip out a fresh, raw, vitamin-filled alternative with an unusual name. It works every time. Fruit is good for your memory and supplies fibre, minerals and antioxidants.

GET FRESH

OK, so you don't have the time or energy to get fresh every day, but a regular diet of processed, ready-made food and takeouts is not good for you. Try to eat fresh, organic (if possible), seasonal food as much as your schedule and budget will allow. Food doesn't have to be cooked. Sushi, for example, is a delicious, healthy option at lunchtime, while raw oysters are an aphrodisiac.

WAITER, MORE WATER PLEASE

Drink alcohol in moderation and designate a number of alcohol-free days every week. Remember how good it feels the next day. Make an effort to drink more water, in between alcoholic drinks and in general. If you do regular exercise, it is important to replenish fluid. And while you are thinking about it, go easy on caffeine drinks.

SOME UNEXPECTED GOOD NEWS

Feeling a bit glum about all this healthy eating business? Have a bit of chocolate. The Ancient Mayans ate chocolate with every meal and research has confirmed that it is nature's own anti-depressant, triggering the release of uplifting hormones. It makes you feel good – now isn't that just the best news?

First Aid and Safety

Now that your home is clean, clutter-free and in good working order, it is time to focus upon what to do in the rather likely event of things going wrong.

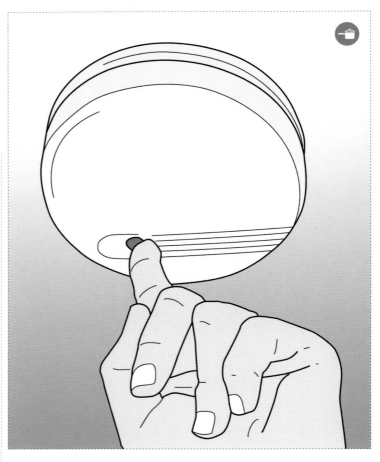

Find out now where to switch off household supplies (e.g. water and electricity) should you still be in the dark on that score. File and store contact numbers for efficient, accredited plumbers and electricians and for the telephone, gas, water and electricity suppliers. Research the important contact names and numbers of your local authority or council. Make sure everyone in the household knows where the information is filed and take responsibility for keeping it up to date. That really friendly plumber you used a couple of years back may by now be enjoying life on a sunny beach somewhere, so flying him back to your home to fix a problem in the bathroom is probably not the best option.

File it

Hold on to receipts from previous household jobs – you may be covered by guarantees for the next time you need work doing. Don't lose contracts and guarantees for household services and appliances, such as the washing machine, refrigerator, computer or four-slice, variable-width toaster you splashed out on. Think ahead. Emergencies happen. Things go wrong, so don't blow a fuse when the fuse blows. Be cool, calm and confident. Be a Domestic God about the house as well as a man around the house. It adds to your appeal. And remember, knowledge is power, so keep it on tap.

Smoke alarms

Ensuring your home is secure is vitally important. Fitting a smoke alarm is up there at the top of the list. It detects smoke or toxic fumes and alerts you to the danger by emitting a very powerful, brain-piercing sound, warning you to make a rapid exit. A smoke alarm is generally easy to fit – follow the manufacturer's instructions to the letter about how and where to install it and how and when to test or change the batteries. Remember to check the mechanism regularly – it can save lives.

DIY appeal

A spot of DIY saves money and time spent waiting for the relevant professional to arrive. Solving household issues with apparent ease can add substantially to your appeal. Try your hand at being a Domestic DIY God. No promises, but at least you can minimize the competition – do you really want to invite a devastatingly handsome plumber into your home to turn heads as well as stopcocks? You've got a blocked toilet under your belt (see page 130) and you could try your hand at a blocked sink, too. If the blockage is due to congealed fat plus various bits of debris, such as tea leaves and coffee grains, try to solve the problem yourself. Don't read your own future, grab it with both hands – in this case around a plunger with a rubber cup large enough to cover the plug hole completely. You can hire one if it is not part of your equipment. Place the rubber section over the plughole and work it up and down strenuously until your efforts are rewarded by a gurgling sound, the complaint from the blockage that you are attempting to evict it without written warning. Having water in the sink as you do this can help by adding pressure. If it does not work, you will have to bail out the water, stand a bucket under the outlet pipe, unscrew the S-bend and await the exit of the offending and often rather offensive squatters. A spoonful of caustic soda in boiling water will cleanse the system and remove anything left behind by the troublemakers. If you detect the cause of the problem, try to avoid pouring it down the sink a second time. If you feel like tackling an outside drain, it's on with the protective gear for your feet, hands and eyes. This is where you may lose out to the handsome plumber so try and do it when your beloved can't see you. It could be that a build up of leaves is the problem so deal with these first. Then remove the metal grid, insert rubber-clad hand and try to remove the cause of the blockage manually. You could use a bit of wire or an old coat hanger to dislodge things. The water should drain away. If it doesn't you may want to call in the experts. Ask for a plain-speaking, plain-looking one if you are very anxious.

KIT FOR CUTS

It's a good idea to collect a few key items to deal with power cuts and other emergencies. Keep them together in a safe place. Make sure all housemates know where the kit is. Ensure it is safe from small two- and four-legged creatures. Here are a few suggestions:

- BATTERY-POWERED TORCHES (KEEP BATTERIES UP TO DATE)
- WIND-UP TORCH (IN CASE YOU DON'T BUY NEW BATTERIES)
- BOX OF MATCHES (MAKE SURE THESE ARE WELL AWAY FROM CHILDREN)
- CANDLES (NEVER LEAVE A LIT CANDLE UNATTENDED)
- SWISS ARMY KNIFE
- BOTTLED WATER

Depending on the emergencies that may be relevant to you, add additional items, such as bottled water, tinned food, a flare, first-aid kit, spare medication etc.

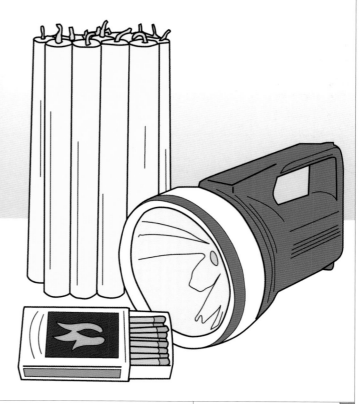

HOW IT WORKS:

The Microwave

T he microwave oven is one of the greatest inventions of the 20th century. The first microwave oven was patented in 1953 and today millions of households contain one. Each year billions of microwave meals are cooked quickly, efficiently and with relatively little mess. Time saved by the microwave can be spent effectively on other household tasks. But just how does this miracle machine work?

1 **CONTAINER:** Microwaves pass through most paper, glass and plastics, so these materials can be used to hold food. However, this is not the case with metal, which reflects the waves, so metal and foil containers should not be used in a microwave.

2 **ROTATING PADDLE:** This scatters the microwaves to ensure they reach all parts of the oven.

3 **MAGNETRON:** The magnetron generates a type of electromagnetic radiation, known as microwaves, which are radiated by an aerial through a metal wave-guide into the oven. There they are scattered by a rotating paddle. Some of the microwaves penetrate the food directly and others are reflected off the walls into the food. This ensures that the food is cooked evenly.

4 **TIMER:** An electronic timing device is used to control the cooking time. A bell sounds when the process is complete. You should wait at least 60 seconds before serving the food in order to avoid the risk of burns or scalds.

5 **PROTECTIVE GRILLE:** A metal screen in the glass door reflects microwaves back into the oven.

6 **TRANSFORMER:** Together with other components, the transformer converts the mains current into a form that can be used by the magnetron.

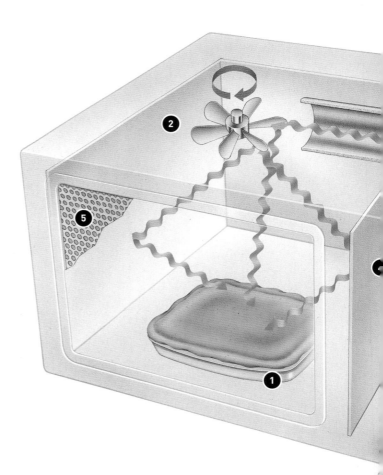

A microwave oven uses high-frequency electronmagnetic waves to heat food. These are radio waves with an electric field that oscillates 2.45 billion times a second. The water molecules within the food have a different electric charge at either end and rotate in time with the changing direction of the electric field. The molecules become excited and the resulting friction and jostling between them generates heat (just like at the office party), thereby cooking the food. Hence the fact that microwave ovens are said to cook food 'from the inside out', whereas in conventional ovens the heat has to migrate from the outside. The microwaves are generated by a magnetron. The magnetron was first developed in World War II for use in radar systems. It was soon discovered that microwaves could penetrate food and the culinary revolution began.

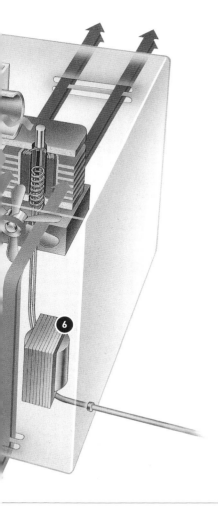

REHEAT A TAKEOUT

Ideally, a takeout should be eaten while still hot. If you decide to eat it later, cover and refrigerate it immediately. Use within one day, reheat it only once and ensure it is served piping hot. You may not be able to see or smell germs, but they are cunning little critters and masters of disguise.

1. Wash hands in hot, soapy water for at least ten seconds. This is an excellent house rule, by the way, for all food preparation.

2. Remove the carton from the refrigerator and transfer contents to a ceramic or glass dish. Aluminium foil containers must not be put in a microwave oven.

3. Cover food with a microwave-safe lid or plastic wrap, taking care that it does not come into direct contact with the food.

4. Halfway through the calculated cooking time, open the door, stir the dish, replace the cover and continue.

5. The bell will sound, indicating it is time to remove the food. Wait for at least 60 seconds before serving.

UTILITY ROOM

Stocked Up
Don't run out of washing powder and cleaning products.

Surfaces
Keep surfaces clean and clear. Sink hygiene is key in the utility room.

Hand wash
Clean your cloths and tea towels every couple of days.

'A CRISP, WELL-PRESSED SHIRT, AND CLEAN, MATCHING SOCKS ARE THE MARK OF A MAN IN CHARGE OF HIS OWN DESTINY.'

Sir Richard Barrons

Equipment Storage
Keep the floor clear of equipment and store it safely. Ensure cleaning products are kept safe from children and pets.

Baskets
Use different baskets for laundry and ironing.

Utility Room

T he utility room is the main engine of the household, its mission to maintain hygiene and safety. Key equipment housed here includes the washing machine, dryer, drying rack, cleaning tools, laundry baskets, ironing board, brushes, brooms, buckets and cloths plus old towels, supplies of toilet paper and materials for recycling. The potential for mess is strong and must be kept to a minimum. Remember, some of the cleaning products may be hazardous if they fall into the wrong hands, so store them carefully, safely and out of the reach of little people and pets. Don't transform your utility room into a futility area.

Here are a few no-nos to help you establish order:

CHORE CHART: WHAT TO DO WHEN

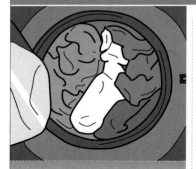  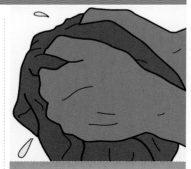

DAILY:
- Tidy surfaces
- Sort laundry
- Clean sink and surfaces
- Trash the trash
- Put wash on overnight

WEEKLY:
- Do ironing (or twice a week)
- Sweep floor
- Check supplies of washing powder and cleaning products

MONTHLY:
- Clean floor thoroughly
- Check equipment in working order
- Handwash woollens
- Search for missing socks

NO-NOS

All the following activities could seriously damage your health:

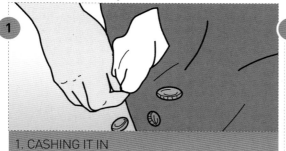

1. CASHING IT IN

Make sure you empty your pockets carefully and thoroughly before putting your jeans (or any other item of clothing equipped with a pocket) into the washing machine. Coins of any dimension and denomination can cause serious damage to the inner workings. Tissues are a no-no unless you enjoy picking their tiny white fragments off your freshly washed dark clothing. If you don't fancy money laundering, don't put notes in either.

2. SMART AND SAFE

The perils of a messy utility room are many and potentially serious. Cleaning products with loose lids can spill their dangerous contents onto the floor, empty containers left lying around can lead you to think they don't need replacing, boxes in the wrong place can trip you up. Store products safely in cupboards above floor level (with childproof locks if necessary). Checking your supplies regularly saves you money in the long run. Establish a home for every item. Allow nothing to squat without permission.

3. DIVIDE AND RULE

One of the keys to successful clothes washing is to sort items into different groups before putting them in the machine: whites stay with whites, darks with darks and non-fast coloureds with non-fast coloureds (i.e. colours that may run). It may sound obvious, but just how many unintentionally baby pink socks, steely grey underwear or blotchy blue T-shirts are out there? Don't let a sneaky bright red sock creep into the white wash. It can infiltrate without being noticed and bring the cleaning process to a very distressing conclusion. Mission accomplished by the sock, but not by you.

4. SAY NO TO OVERFLOW

Don't let laundry pile up and overwhelm both you and the utility room. Deal with dirty washing on a regular basis. Have one basket for dirty clothes and another for clean items in need of ironing. Choose different coloured baskets to avoid confusion. Think how upset you would be to discover you had spent all evening ironing your partner's entire collection of dirty shirts. Fold clean clothes neatly to minimize ironing. Do one load of washing overnight and another first thing the next morning to keep up with a large backlog.

The Laundry Affair:
Love Your Washing Machine

O k guys, it's time to get intimate with your washing machine. Whether you have a utility room dedicated to the arduous task of keeping your clothes clean and an outside space in which to dry them naturally, or have to make do with a corner of your kitchen and a couple of radiators, your life will become immeasurably easier if you form a deep and lasting relationship with your machine. It's time to commit. Those of you looking for a let-out can opt for disposable underwear and a new shirt every day, spend evenings in the launderette, or visit your mother every weekend.

Accumulate to speculate

It makes sense to accumulate a sizeable washing load in order to make the most efficient use of your washing machine. However, be careful not to pack the machine too full – you'll strain the works. Establish a routine of laundering at least once a week. Choose a night when there's more on the screen than in your diary. As your washing piles up, sort it into different colours to save you time later. Read on to find out how.

Why the label?

Labels are attached to your clothes for a reason – they are not merely design features, but are meant to be read. Ever heard of a designer called Hand Wash? OK it's tedious, but paying close attention to a label prevents accidents and preserves your favourite shirt in some semblance of its original state. Examining and digesting the label enables you to sort the laundry into appropriate piles according to fabric type, colour-fastness and dirt level. Wash those items that require a similar treatment together. There's quite a bit to learn – the choice of different natural and manmade fabrics available is quite wide and there's a recommendation for each one. Follow it to the letter and you could end up with 20 piles of just three items, a nightmare for the time and motion man you have now become! Clearly, a little compromise is called for. To make the laundry load more manageable, sort it as follows: First, separate it into two piles of items requiring hand and machine washing, then sub-divide the machine washing into three piles: cottons and linen; synthetics; delicates/wool. This should result in four piles, but now you must bring colour into the equation.

Don't wear rose-tinted spectacles

It's important to wash dark and light colours separately and to keep non-fast and colourfast items apart. Some colours are prone to run when immersed in water and will bleed into other items in the wash. Non-colourfast items need to be washed separately or with like colours. Denim jeans are notorious for losing colour, even when they are sold faded or pre-washed. Check the label to see whether an item is colourfast. Some bright colours are prone to fading, so with time your favourite blue shirt could become a shadow of its former self. To avoid this, soak in a bowl of cold water and salt.

The Enigma machine

You don't have to be an undercover spy to decipher the codes on the dials of your washing machine, but it might help. It is very important to follow your machine's guidelines when choosing a cycle but the following information may help – it's just a general guide though, so remember that washing cycles and recommended temperatures vary from machine to machine. If you are washing several items together that require different temperatures, go for the lowest temperature recommended on the care labels.

Cottons and linen

The machine cycle for washing these fabrics is lengthy and the temperature very hot (60-95°C). Watch out for the vigorous washing action with a high-speed spin. It's like a Formula One event – hot, fast and action-packed. Higher temperatures are normally suitable for white cottons and linen without special finishes, while coloured linen without special finishes and colourfast cottons should be washed at a cooler temperature. Non-colourfast cottons should be washed at an even cooler temperature.

Synthetics

The synthetic fabric cycle is shorter, less vigorous and cooler (generally around 40-50°C) with a slower spin speed. It suits nylon, polyester, polyester/cotton, viscose, acrylic blends, linen and acetate, but do note that some synthetics require the delicates cycle so check the label. This cycle is like a nervous warm up for the big race – slower laps, less action.

Delicates and wool

This cycle is the shortest, with a gentler washing action, a cooler water temperature (30-40°C) and a low-spin speed. It is suitable for machine-washable wool and wool blends, machine-washable silks, some synthetics and very delicate items such as that lace tablecloth your aunt gave you for some reason. It's like a vintage car rally, where style wins over speed, but accidents can cause bad damage.

A GUIDE TO CLOTHES CARE SYMBOLS

WASHING

COTTON WASH
(MAXIMUM)

SYNTHETICS WASH
(MEDIUM)

WOOL WASH
(MINIMUM)

HAND WASH
ONLY

DO NOT WASH

The temperature in the wash tub symbol is the maximum recommended wash temperature for that item

DRY CLEANING

MAY BE DRY
CLEANED

MAY BE DRY
CLEANED (LETTERS
ARE FOR THE DRY
CLEANER)

DO NOT
DRY CLEAN

BLEACHING

CHLORINE BLEACH
MAY BE USED

DO NOT USE
CHLORINE-BASED
BLEACH

DRYING

DO NOT
TUMBLE DRY

TUMBLE DRY
(LOW SETTING)

TUMBLE DRY
(HIGH SETTING)

TUMBLE DRY

DRY FLAT

HANG DRY

DRIP DRY

IRONING

COOL IRON –
ACRYLIC, NYLON,
POLYESTER

WARM IRON –
POLYESTER
MIXTURES, WOOL

HOT IRON –
COTTON, LINEN,
VISCOSE

DO NOT IRON

Loading the Machine

You may think that life is too short to calculate the weight of your boxer shorts and shirts as they are fed into your washing machine, however most handbooks recommend maximum loads of around 4-5 kg (8.8-11lbs) for cottons and 2-2.5kg (4½-5½lbs) for synthetics. What's the reason for the difference? The rubbing action of robust fabrics against one other helps to clean them, so sturdy cottons will benefit from getting up close and personal, but not so those delicates and synthetics. However, overload the machine and it will not wash effectively. It may become unbalanced and moonwalk across the floor, so make sure there is enough space to fit your hand in at the top of a front loader.

Use the recommended quantities of detergent – too much and things will get very bubbly. It may look funny, like in the cartoons, but you won't get any credit until you have mopped up the mess.

Zip, pin, fasten

Close zips, fasten loose buttons and place clothes with attachments (such as a buckle) in a pillowcase to avoid damage to other items. Remove detachable items such as pins or cufflinks.

Zap the dirt – the secrets of pre-washing

If things have got really dirty, try a spot of pre-wash soaking. You can buy special products for this, but a long soak for several hours in water and mild detergent may help. Stains should be treated separately before washing – either with a special stain-removing product or by spot cleaning. Read the manufacturer's instructions and if you are unsure about the suitability of any stain remover, test it first on an inconspicuous area. You can also spot-clean areas such as collars and cuffs by moistening a bar of soap and rubbing across the offending areas, then brushing or scrubbing lightly with a nail brush to loosen the dirt. Take care not to damage the fabric by scrubbing too vigorously. Some delicate fabrics, such as silk, do not take kindly to spot cleaning and could fade or show a watermark. Stains such as blood and egg are best soaked in cool water, as hot water tends to fix them. Many washing machines also have a pre-wash cycle for heavily soiled items.

Detergents

For woollen items and hand washing, use small (or recommended) quantities of a gentle, mild detergent rather than the stronger one you normally use for the bulk of your machine wash. Some mild detergents are suitable for both machine- and hand-washing but others work best when used for hand washing only.

Biological detergents contain enzymes that help remove protein stains such as blood, egg, grass and dairy products. They are usually safe for most washable fabrics, except silk and wool, and for delicate items. However, if your (or your partner's) skin is sensitive to biological detergents and you get an allergic reaction, use a milder non-biological detergent. 'Automatic' detergents produce fewer suds and should only be used in a washing machine.

Fabric conditioners

Imagine how the resumé of a fabric conditioner would read. It would state one definite skill as 'caring for fabrics by making them softer and easier to iron' while hobbies include 'the prevention of static electricity'. A definite no-no would be to use a conditioner for silk or towels though. Don't use it in every wash either, or you may get an unwanted build up of grease. Pop a softener sheet in the dryer from time to time for a smoother result. Keep odours at bay in the laundry basket with a conditioner sheet.

X BLEACH – HANDLE WITH CARE

Chlorine bleach is strong stuff and should never be used on delicate fabrics or materials such as wool, silk and nylon. It can whiten whites, brighten colourfast items and remove some stains. However, frequent bleaching can weaken and damage fabric. Oxygen bleach is generally suitable for use on most fabrics and will help maintain whiteness and brightness of colour. Just remember to use it occasionally rather than relying on it as part of your regular stain-removing kit.

HOUSEHOLD MANAGEMENT FOR **MEN**

HOT AND BUBBLY

Time equals stain ▶

The longer a soiled item remains unwashed, the harder it is to remove the dirt and the smellier it will become. Dirt plus time equals stubborn, smelly stain.

Hot is best ▶

The hotter the water, the more effectively it cleans. However, the hotter the water, the more it is likely to shrink a garment and cause fading, or different colours to bleed into one another.

Fluffy towels ▶

New towels are particularly prone to depositing fluff around the place, so may need to be washed separately for the first few times.

Do it by hand ▶

Machine-washable woollens are a great invention – no more struggling with water-logged knitwear that weighs a ton. Nevertheless, knitwear is notorious for shrinking. If the label does not specify machine washing, don't risk it – wash the item by hand, or your nice new jumper could end up fitting your teddy bear better than you.

Storage ▶

Store dirty laundry in a container such as a wicker basket, where air will circulate well.

Dry first ▶

Don't place wet or damp towels and clothes in the laundry basket – dry them first, or mildew will gatecrash the scene and set off stink bombs.

Don't delay ▶

Never leave items in the machine once the cycle has finished, otherwise you risk creasing, odour and mildew. Yuk.

Scrape first ▶

The laundry may have labels attached to it, but unlike vintage wine it does not mature with age. Before washing clothes, remove as much loose dirt as possible by scraping off mud and other dried substances.

Inside out ▶

If you wish to prevent jeans from fading, turn them inside out. Ditto items with a pile, such as corduroy or velvet.

Match up ▶

Wash matching items together, so any fading that occurs is uniform.

Bag up ▶

You may want to wash small items such as socks or handkerchiefs in a thin cloth bag or pillowcase, but ensure you secure the end so that they cannot escape during washing. Otherwise the lost sock syndrome will set in. Using a safety pin to keep socks together maintains their beautiful partnership.

Handwashing: Gently Does It

Handwashing is generally reserved for delicate fabrics such as silks, wools and items that bleed colour. Check the care label for temperature recommendation. Cool or tepid water is around 30°C, warm 40°C and hot 60°C. If an item loses its colour easily, use cool or cold water. Very delicate fabrics should be soaked in lukewarm water for several minutes and then lifted and gently dipped in and out of the water several times – pretend you are a backing singer to create rhythm for this motion. Rinse in cool or cold water using the same action as for washing until all the detergent is removed and the fabric stops feeling slippery. Never wring out a very delicate item, as this can weaken and damage the fabric. Instead, gently squeeze out the excess water. The washing action for more robust items can be more vigorous. Perfect a squeezing and releasing action to force water through the material and thereby loosen the dirt. Rub the fabric gently against itself. If you're hand-washing because you simply can't cram any more into the washing machine or if your trusted companion (i.e. the machine, not your mother or your partner) is unwell, different rules apply and, depending on the fabric, your washing action can be more aggressive. Give soiled areas a vigorous scrub with a brush.

Drying

For city dwellers, drying may be restricted to suspending a drying rack over the bath or a bout of tumble-drying (label permitting). If you are lucky enough to have an outside space, take advantage of it to give your clothes a chance to get out in the fresh air.

The great outdoors

Clothes dried outside will benefit from a natural airing and smell much nicer, provided you don't live next door to an industrial plant belching out smoke, or a major five-lane highway. Make sure you run a damp cloth along the washing line to remove any dirt before pegging out the clothes. Birds like to hang out on lines and are less domesticated than you (hopefully). Shake the clothes to remove as many creases as possible, smooth them out and peg on the line, placing pegs on the seams or inconspicuous parts – you don't want unwelcome bumps in strategic points. All of these actions will save ironing time. Strong sunlight can bleach white cotton and linen and return it to its former glory, bringing back sunshine into your wash. It can also fade deeply coloured clothes, so you may want to dry some of these items in the shade or hang them inside out. Delicate items and knitwear (coaxed gently back into shape) can be dried flat on a clean, colourfast towel or on a drying rack. Peg woollens by the hem or you will look as if you are smuggling hangers. Hang trousers by the waistband, shirts by the tails, towels, sheets and tea towels loosely by the corners and socks in pairs. It's as easy as that.

Grab your gear off the line while still damp in the unlikely but recommended event of a scheduled no-delay attack on the ironing. If unfeasible, remove washing when dry and place, folded neatly, in to the ironing basket.

Indoors

Drying clothes in direct contact with a heat source can cause shrinking and damage to delicate fabrics. Dry clothes on a rack close to a radiator rather than on it. Remember to remove these items before guests arrive. Getting to know your underwear on a first date is never advisable.

Lightweight delicate fabrics such as silk can be hung up to drip dry, but other delicate fabrics that may stretch when wet, including knitwear, should be reshaped and dried flat on a clean, colourfast towel or on a drying frame. Shirts and jackets can be dried on hangers either indoors or out, but make sure you use a hanger with broad shoulders rather than a wire one.

The tumble dryer

Manufacturer's guidelines are important when it comes to tumble driers. Many fabrics can be placed in a dryer but certain synthetics, such as acetate and acrylics, delicate items and some knitwear cannot. Follow the care labels' recommendations. Drying at too hot a temperature can leave things smaller and more yellow than before and in some cases, melted like the cheese on a burger. Sort items for drying as for washing, and ensure light colours are separated from dark and colourfast from non-colourfast. Generally, items that are suitable for machine-washing together are suitable for drying together. Sturdy cottons and linen can normally withstand a hot temperature while synthetics and delicates need a lower one, but as ever there are exceptions, so do read those care labels. For fabrics that deposit fluff, items with decoration, tangling shirt sleeves etc., you can also follow the same rules as for washing. Always shake out and untangle items before placing them in the dryer to help the warm air circulate and prevent a Houdini effect. More brain now means less brawn on the ironing board later – focus on that if the spirits are flagging. Fabric-softener sheets can be used with synthetic fabrics in the dryer to cut down on static electricity, but they may leave a waxy coating on towels and sheets. Remove items as soon as they are dry and hang or fold them carefully to minimize ironing. Folding is like moisturizing – it protects against unwanted wrinkles.

Clean fluff off your dryer with a paintbrush.

HANG IT ALL

Hang your clothes carefully and as soon after washing as possible. If you wear it on the top half, hang it from the bottom. If you wear it on the bottom half, hang it from the top.

1 SHEETS
Fold sheets hem to hem and then fold a hand's length over the line. Peg corners. It should look rather like a hammock that's mated with a snail.

2 SHIRTS
Stretch out the shirt as shown and peg. Share a peg with the next shirt for efficient use of line space.

3 PANTS AND BOXERS
Peg at the waist – a small request for smalls that don't want unsightly pinch marks in awkward places.

4 TOWELS
Give the towel a good shake before hanging up and pegging, again folding a hand's length over the line.

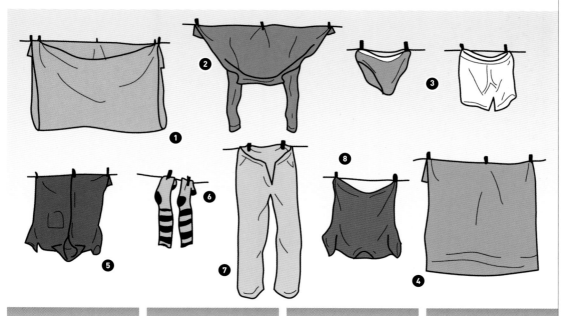

5 SHORT SLEEVE SHIRT
Hang by the tails or you'll get peg marks on the shoulders.

6 SOCKS
Peg by the toes and keep them in line on the line, or they won't march in step.

7 TROUSERS
Peg the waist, don't waste the peg. Turn a bit of the material over for extra security.

8 T-SHIRT
It's bottoms up for T-shirts, too.

Stain Solutions

I f you don't want your clothes to act as a visual record of shaving cuts, post-pub takeouts and mishaps with a dipstick, you'll be pleased to hear that there are several commercial products out there to zap the tell-tale reminders of a good night out. Stain removers in stick form are good for grimy collars and cuffs, but if you want to try rustling up something a little more homespun, or no shop-bought solutions are to hand, here are a few suggestions for beating common stains on washable fabrics.

The treatment of a stain depends on its cause and, as usual, there are a few golden rules to follow. This will come as no surprise to those of you who have read the previous section on laundry diligently:

■ Check the care label and if it recommends dry cleaning only, whisk it off to the nearest cleaners.

■ Don't hang around. Speed counts. A fresh stain is a vulnerable stain, timorous and unsure of itself. Strike quickly, and you may still be able to talk it round and persuade it to leave your trousers in peace. Leave it to mature and it may become so entrenched and set in its ways that it becomes an unwelcome reminder of things past.

■ Make sure you use a white or pale coloured cloth (and this even applies to kitchen towels) for working on the stain. You don't want a pink tinge from your old red t-shirt added to that interesting khaki-coloured curry stain on your trousers.

■ If you are unsure how a fabric will respond to a stain buster, commercial or home-made, try it on an inconspicuous part of the fabric or garment first, such as the inside of a pocket, or the reverse of a seam.

■ It may be stating the obvious, but remember to mop up any excess stain first with a clean cloth or absorbent kitchen towel, or scrape off excess with a blunt-edged knife.

■ So as not to spread the stain to another part of the fabric, or to make it more absorbed by the fabric itself, spread the affected area, reverse side up, over a clean cloth or kitchen towel. This will enable you to work at the stain from the inside out.

■ Work on the stain from the outer edge towards the centre.

THE A-Z OF STAIN REMOVALS

BLOOD
Soak bloodstains in cold salty water for at least 30 minutes, but strike fast while the stain is still fresh. Then soak in a solution of biological detergent and wash as usual. If the stains are older, dilute a little ammonia in cold water and dab the stain, then wash as usual.

GREASE STAINS
(Butter, margarine, mayonnaise, cooking oil etc.)
Prepare a paste using a little bicarbonate of soda and water and apply to the stain for 30 minutes. Next, soak the fabric in warm water to which a mild detergent has been added. Or soak in a biological detergent for a minimum of 30 minutes, and up to several hours, depending upon how old the stain is. This is one instance where you can wash in the hottest water that the fabric can withstand.

CANDLEWAX
Remove as much excess wax as possible with a blunt knife. Place the stained area between two sheets of brown paper – keep the absorbent (slighly fluffy) sides of the paper adjacent to the fabric and iron over the stain with a warm iron. The wax will adhere to the paper. Repeat with clean parts of the paper until the wax has been removed. Or place the stain between two kitchen towels and press with a warm iron.

CHEWING GUM
Place the item in a plastic bag in the freezer. Once the gum has hardened it can be chipped off. Or hold the gummed area over a steaming kettle (watch your fingers) until the gum softens enough to pull off carefully. Remove any remaining gum with a little white spirit on a clean cloth.

CHOCOLATE
Dab with lukewarm water to which a detergent has been added, or with a simple solution of borax (25g) and cold water (600ml), or wash with a biological detergent.

CURRY
Curry stains are tough. Try soaking in warm water, changing the water if it becomes coloured by the curry. Squeeze out the excess water and dab on a mixture of glycerine and water (combined in equal quantities), leave for an hour, rinse and repeat if necessary, then wash in a biological detergent.

EGG

Try soaking egg stains (having scraped off as much excess egg as possible) in a simple solution of borax and water (see Chocolate) or in salty water. Alternatively, soak raw egg stains in biological detergent and then wash as usual. Cooked egg stains can be soaked in salty water, rinsed, then soaked in plain water and washed as usual. Or soak in a biological detergent.

GRASS

Are parts of your cricket whites green? Washing in a biological detergent should remove most grass stains, but if badly stained, soak in a solution of ordinary washing soda (55g) and warm water (2.5l), then rinse. Or dab with methylated spirits before washing.

LIPSTICK AND OIL

For post-dinner-party lipstick stains on your posh white cloth napkins or nasty brushes with a bicycle chain, raid an aromatherapy kit for some eucalyptus oil. Dab on a few drops and leave for a few minutes before washing as usual. Or dab the stain with a cloth soaked in white spirit and then wash as usual.

OIL-BASED PAINT

Dab gently with a clean cloth soaked in white spirit, rinse and wash as usual.

PERSPIRATION

Soak in warm water to which a handful of bicarbonate of soda has been added. 1-2 tablespoons of lemon juice or white vinegar can be used in place of the soda. Or sponge with a solution of ammonia (5ml) and water (500ml), rinse immediately and wash as usual.

INK

Ballpoint and felt-tip pen stains caused by non-permanent inks may be easily removed by washing as normal. Treat stains caused by permanent inks by rubbing gently with a cotton bud dipped in methylated spirits, then wash as usual.

RED OR DARK FRUIT, BEETROOT, OLD RED WINE

Soak the stain in a small dish of glycerine for around 30 minutes and then rinse with water. Alternatively, pour hot water from a height over the stain and allow to drain through the fabric. The height and friction often loosens the stain. This is an exception to the rule (eyes right).

RED WINE

The old barmaid's tale of pouring white wine over red wine that has been spilled on a carpet is not to be sneezed at. Be generous with the white, leave to soak for 10-15 minutes and rinse with lukewarm water. For older stains, see Red Fruit. Another tried and tested solution is to cover the entire stain generously in salt to absorb as much of the wine as possible, leave for several hours, brush off, soak in biological detergent and then wash as usual.

RUST

Mix one heaped tablespoon of table salt in the juice of one lemon and soak the stain in this solution for one hour, rinse and then wash as usual. Dry in the sun if the colour of the fabric will not be harmed by the bleaching action of strong sunlight. Repeat as necessary.

SHOE POLISH

Dab with white spirit and wash as usual.

TEA AND COFFEE

Dab glycerine onto the stain and work in with a clean cloth, rinse with warm water. Or, soak in a biological detergent and then wash as usual.

VOMIT

Scrape off the excess, rinse in cold water and soak in water to which a biological detergent has been added, then wash as usual. And don't do it again.

DOMESTIC GOD

That most innocent and abundant of liquids, H_2O – or water to the non-chemists among you – is one of the best weapons in your stain-busting armoury. However, make sure that you use only lukewarm or even cold water, (unless treating a stain caused by grease or fats) as hot water can fix a stain, leaving it as a shining testament to your sloppy eating habits. Also avoid tumble drying a stained item and take care not to iron over a stained area, unless you have given up on trying to remove it – again the heat could set the stain.

Ironing Out Your Problems

A s you read this, you may be sporting a nicely ironed cotton shirt with smart cuffs and an immaculate, wrinkle-free collar. If so, be honest, did you iron it? It may be that you have gone for a permanent-press, wrinkle-resistant model. Is that your ideal choice? Perhaps you are wearing no shirt at all but, instead, an outfit made of 100 per cent polyester or an ensemble that hasn't seen an ironing board in years. Do you have an ironing board? Look around for a long tapered object with collapsible legs and a pointed end (no, that's your housemate). It's time to get a few things straight.

A pressing issue

Ironing is not the most enjoyable part of household management, it has to be said. Think of it as the equivalent of your least favourite task in the office or at college. However, its execution leaves you smarter, sharper, harder-edged than the competition. You will look as if you mean business, proceeding towards your target in defined, straight lines. Have a go. It's not that bad.

A few basics are required:

- An ironing board (or a suitable hard surface that is not heat-sensitive and over which you can spread a smooth, secure, clean and heat-resistant cover). Don't even think about the antique dining table.

- An iron (duh) – make sure that it is absolutely clean underneath. If there are deposits or the scorched remains of your last attempt on the soleplate (undercarriage), they will transfer onto your clothing. Test both cleanliness and heat on an inconspicuous area of the item of clothing to avoid meltdown, scorched fabric or overheated tempers.

- A can of spray starch (for cotton shirts) – one of life's little miracles.

- Water – to sprinkle on clothes that are too dry (unless you have a steam iron, of course). You can sprinkle by hand or put water in a spray bottle.

- A preliminary laundry sort – work through the 'temperature range' of your ironing pile, which will no doubt be made up of different fabric types, each one requiring a different temperature setting – lowest first for synthetics and silks, finishing up with the high temperatures for linen and cotton.

X NO-NOS BEFORE YOU START

- IRONS GET HOT. DON'T TOUCH THE SOLEPLATE OR YOU WILL BURN YOURSELF. IT MAY SOUND OBVIOUS BUT PEOPLE DO IT.

- NEVER, EVER IRON A PIECE OF CLOTHING WHILE WEARING IT. HUMANS DON'T COME WITH CARE LABELS.

- DON'T WALK OUT OF THE ROOM LEAVING THE IRON SWITCHED ON.

LET'S GET DOWN TO IT
Check, check, check
Treat ironing like an operation. Be on your metal.

1. **Check** that your ironing board is at the right height. Whether you like to do it sitting down or standing up, you should be able to place your palms on the board without having to bend either arm or back.

2. **Check** the manufacturer's recommendations on the clothes label and set the temperature accordingly. Decode the dot temperature system on your iron as follows: one dot for cool (low temperatures – synthetics), two dots for warm (medium temperature – silk and wool) and three dots for hot (high temperature – cotton and linen). If a fabric is blended, set the temperature according to the most delicate fabric in the blend. If there are no dots, it is probably a toy one.

3. **Check** whether you should iron a particular fabric inside out or not. Inside out is best for velvet, acrylic and corduroy, plus embroidered clothes and synthetic leathers. Silk, rayon and wool should also be ironed on the wrong side with a pressing cloth (a clean white tea towel or napkin is fine) over the top. Placing a clean towel or blanket on the ironing board itself helps to avoid unwanted sheen. For the same reason, it's a good idea to iron other fabrics on the wrong side, e.g. dark cottons and linens.

TIME-SAVING TECHNIQUES

- IF YOU HANG UP WET CLOTHES PROPERLY, THEY WILL LOOK SMOOTHER WHEN DRY AND LESS IN NEED OF AN IRON. FOLD CLOTHES IMMEDIATELY AFTER REMOVING FROM THE DRYER AND DON'T DUMP THEM IN A LAUNDRY BASKET FOR DAYS ON END.
- THERE'S NO REAL NEED TO IRON UNDERWEAR, HANDKERCHIEFS, TEA TOWELS, TOWELS, SWEATPANTS AND SWEATSHIRTS.
- IF YOU FEEL COMPELLED TO IRON TEA TOWELS AND HANDKERCHIEFS, DO TWO OR THREE AT A TIME.
- SMOOTH DOWN YOUR JEANS BY HAND, THEY DON'T REALLY NEED IRONING.
- ONLY IRON THE VISIBLE SIDE OF A DUVET COVER.

IRONING A SHIRT

OK, now you've been briefed, you're ready for action. First mission – a shirt (your best one may be too ambitious). Place it on the board, smooth it out with your hand, and go for it. Bear in mind that circular motions can damage material, so use a back-and-forth stroke, with only a slight downward pressure. It's the heat not the force that removes wrinkles. Remember to iron first the parts that are extra thick, such as collars, cuffs, sleeves and pockets – they will wrinkle less as you tackle the remainder.

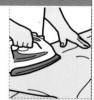

1. Start with the collar, wrong side first: work towards the ends and then back to the centre, using short strokes. Repeat on the right side. After ironing, fold the collar down and crease with your hand, not the iron.

2. Now the shoulder yoke: smooth the yoke by slipping one shoulder over the narrow end of the board, ironing from the shoulder to the centre of the back. Repeat on the other side.

3. Cuffs next: iron inside and then outside.

4. Sleeves to follow: iron the body of each sleeve, starting with the cuff opening. Then iron reverse side. Some people like to use a sleeve board on top of the ironing board.

5. Finish with the body: iron the shirt body, beginning with one front panel and continuing with the other. Nose the iron gently around the buttons. If you iron buttons, they may well melt.

IRONING TROUSERS

1. POCKETS:
PULL OUT POCKETS, PUT ON THE BOARD AND IRON

2. WAISTLINE:
FIT THE WAISTLINE AROUND THE IRONING BOARD. IRON THE TOP OF THE TROUSERS, ROTATING THE GARMENT AWAY FROM YOUR BODY.

3. LEGS (INSIDE):
LAY TROUSERS FLAT, ONE LEG ON TOP OF THE OTHER. LINE UP THE INSEAMS BY MATCHING THE SIDES OF EACH LEG. IRON THE INSIDE OF THE BOTTOM LEG BY FOLDING BACK THE TOP LEG. FLIP AND REPEAT ON THE OTHER SIDE.

4. LEGS (OUTSIDE):
KEEP THE INSEAMS LINED UP AND IRON THE OUTSIDE OF EACH LEG.

5. HANG IT ALL:
HANG UP IMMEDIATELY

Help!

I want perfect creases – help!
Iron the crease and set with a boost of steam.

I've got horrid seam marks on my seams – help!
Rub gently with a slightly damp, clean sponge or tea towel.

Ironing wool – a pressing problem

1. Place a clean, colourfast towel under the wool garment (once it is totally dry and has been turned inside out).

2. Press (rather than iron) using steam or a damp pressing cloth and your iron at a medium temperature. Pressing means what it says – applying pressure with the iron without moving it back and forth. Otherwise the woollen item may develop bulges in all the wrong places. Avoid direct contact with the iron or unwanted sheen will appear.

3. Fold rather than hang the finished garment.

Help!

The cat slept on my tie all night. How do i iron it – help!
If you are ironing a silk tie, do so on the wrong (under) side with a dry pressing cloth on top.

I've got horrid marks on my soleplate – help!
If spray starch sticks to the base of the iron, remove with a specialist commercial cleaner or (if you fancy making your own remedy) a paste of bicarbonate of soda and water on the tip of an old but clean toothbrush. Rub till clean. Wipe off any residue.

My iron is all clogged up – help!
Check the instructions – it could be that you should be using distilled water in the tank of your iron.

I've got candle wax on my trousers and on the tablecloth and on the carpet – help!
Pick off large pieces by hand and iron over the remains through kitchen paper. Go easy on the candles! What were you doing?

I can't do ironing – help!
Yes, you can. It takes practice but you will soon come to love your iron.

Ironing is sooo boring. What can i do to make it more interesting?
Listen to a CD or audio book. Don't watch television or you will re-design your shirts.

I always have a huge pile of ironing. What can i do about it?
A little a day keeps the dry cleaners away. Keep up with your load by doing one night a week at the ironing board. Otherwise you will run out of shirts for work, college or a big date. Hang in there or become King of Polyester.

DOMESTIC GOD

Ironing wool or dark fabric trousers can create a shiny look. To avoid unwanted sheen, use a clean tea towel or pressing cloth. Do not iron plastic, nylon or polyester zips. They will melt and leave you undone.

The Washing Machine

A Washing machines come in top- or front-loading designs. They tend to be front-loading in the UK (except in launderettes) and top-loading in the USA and Australia. Front-loaders use less water and energy and fit neatly under worktops. Water and detergent is agitated by the rotating action of the ribbed drum inside making for a more gentle clean. Top-loaders meanwhile boss the clothes about with spinning paddles. They're generally larger in size, meaning they can take bigger loads and are also easier to access.

Due to life-changing microchip technology, both types of machines can be adjusted according to the size of the load, the chosen temperature of the wash and the rinse water, the length of the cycle, the speed of the spin and the number of rinses. They can deal with a whole range of fabrics. Today's washing machines work in combination with the modern detergents, which were developed in the mid-20th century. These synthetic chemicals lift dirt and grease from fabrics with ease.

Machine manufacturers also devised ways of drying clothes more quickly. Spin dryers that expelled the water from the clothes using a rapidly-spinning, perforated drum were making life even easier by the 1920s. In the 1950s, tumble dryers were introduced, drying the clothes in a slowly rotating drum through which heated air is passed. The hot air absorbs moisture and is then vented through a duct or condensing unit. Some washing machines include spin-drying and tumble-drying functions and are great space-savers.

Front-loading washer-dryer

When the timer switches on, inlet valves are opened and water and detergent are sprayed into the drum. When full the drum rotates, washing the clothes. The pump removes dirty water. The valves then admit clean water, rinsing the clothes. Rapid spinning of the drum forces water out of the clothes. Finally, hot air dries the clothes.

How detergent works

Some dirt dissolves in water and rinses out of clean clothes, but greasy or oily stains do not, so additional cleaning agents are necessary to remove them. Modern detergents are specifically designed to perform this task and, unlike soap, do not leave scum in hard water. One end of the detergent molecule is acidic and is attracted to water molecules; the other, a hydrocarbon chain, is repelled by water molecules and is attracted to oil molecules. See page 138 for a visual explanation of this process. It's the same principle with soap on skin and detergent on clothes. But don't be tempted to climb in the machine for a quick wash. You won't fit.

The science of clean clothes
Detergent molecule

The acidic end of a detergent molecule bonds to water and the hydrocarbon end is repelled by water.

Surrounding the stains

The water-repellent ends of the detergent molecules are attracted to oily stains. Gradually, the detergent molecules build up around the stain until the dirt is surrounded by detergent.

Dissolving oil and grease

The detergent-surrounded particles can no longer adhere to the fabric and so float free. The water-bonding ends of the detergent molecules dissolve in water, and the oily particles get rinsed away.

LIVING AREA

Clutter
Don't allow old newspapers to clutter surfaces. Yesterday is old news. File magazines and books. Prune your collection regularly.

Surfaces
Tidy, dust and polish table tops.

Foliage
An easy-care cactus adds colour and height to a room and enjoys the warm, dry atmosphere.

'A PLACE FOR EVERYTHING AND
EVERYTHING IN ITS PLACE.'

William Morris

Urban Chic
A sofa tray makes eating in the living area both safe and sofa-sticated.

Floors
Keep floors clear of clutter and vacuum regularly.

Plant Life
Clean your plant's leaves carefully and water regularly, according to needs.

Smart, Tidy Living Area

Take a look around your living area. What do you see? If all you can take in are clean surfaces, organized piles of recent magazines, empty waste paper bins, tidy rows of books, neatly stored CDs, videos and DVDs, then congratulations, you are in a clutter-free zone. The chances are though, that you will need a good clear out.

In the living area, clutter is a vampire that eats time. If left unchecked, it also steals space and energy, and can become oppressive, draining you of physical and emotional vitality. The very sight of too much mess and clutter may even drain you of all motivation to tidy up. Luckily though, it's relatively easy to stop things piling up.

CHORE CHART: WHAT TO DO WHEN

DAILY:
- Tidy table tops and floors
- Wipe dirty surfaces
- Trash or recycle newspapers
- Tidy away books and magazines
- Put away cds and videos
- Clear dirty cups and plates
- Remove leftover food and
- Empty cans
- Empty wastepaper baskets
- Plump up cushions
- Find and display remote controls

WEEKLY:
- Sweep or vacuum floors,
- Rugs and carpets thoroughly
- Dust all surfaces
- Polish wooden furniture
- Clean glass surfaces thoroughly
- Polish mirrors
- Keep fireplace clean
- Replace flowers
- Organize cds and videos
- Have quick declutter

MONTHLY:
- Dust or vacuum walls
- Dust and clean ceiling fans
- Vacuum sofas and cushions
- Wash windows
- Clean fireplace thoroughly
- Sort magazines – file or trash
- Dust plants
- Dust lamp shades
- Dust blinds
- Dust door tops
- Check smoke alarm

X NO-NOS

Say goodbye to clutter and hello to hygiene. In the pursuit of a clutter-free, clean and positive living space, homeless is hopeless, so get rid of these common offenders:

1. DIRTY DISHES

Among the worst clutter culprits in the living area are dirty dishes, malodorous remains of take-outs and snacks, beer cans (half-emptied or squashed to a pulp), full or even partly full, used cups and glasses and anything that comes under the 'unwashed and lonely' heading. Clear away after you have finished eating – don't let dirty dishes languish in the living area. Deal with the packaging as soon as you have finished your meal – put it in the trash or recycling box.

2. DISCARDED CLOTHES

It's all too easy to leave coats, sweaters, dirty handkerchiefs, discarded socks and 'look what I had for breakfast' ties lying around in the living area in a 'can't be bothered, just off to bed' kind of manner. Don't do it, otherwise you'll soon find half the contents of your wardrobe piled high in the living room and an empty laundry basket elsewhere in the house. Homeless items of clothing don't make a good impression on partners or guests. This is a living area, not a lost and found office.

3. HALF FULL OR HALF EMPTY

Unless you have an unusual penchant for cold, congealed coffee, don't leave sad and forgotten cups on the table or floor as if part of a scientific experiment or strange still life painting. That nasty rim of milk can cause some serious surface tension. Get a handle on the issue and take used cups into the kitchen where they belong. Don't let them leave unsightly stains on the furniture. It only makes more work for you or the housework fairies.

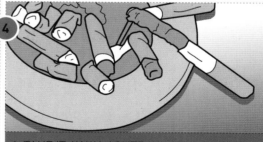

4. TAKE IT AWAY, ASHTRAY

Dirty, overflowing and stained ashtrays are absolute no-nos. Their lack of visual appeal is just one of their crimes. Other offences that need to be taken into consideration include offensive odours and health hazards. One sneeze and the ash is airborne. One clumsy guest and the contents are everywhere. If you feel like a smoke, think of other folk. Don't let nasty ashtrays squat in the living area alongside empty cigarette packets. Open the windows. Let in the fresh air.

De-junking Your Space

Y ou will know that clutter has reached dangerous levels when you trip over a pile of old newspapers, slide headlong across a forgotten glossy magazine sprawled on the floor, or spend half an hour looking for your house keys and credit cards first thing in the morning when you have an important meeting to go to. What you need is a concerted attack on the clutter, some useful storage and a reduced level of sloppiness for a more ordered existence.

Cut the clutter
Everything we bring through our front door needs a storage place (either temporary or permanent) or a place in the trash, so here's how to deal with most of the stuff.

Uncontrolled collecting, unnecessary hoarding and sheer laziness when it comes to containing piles of stuff are all enemies of a tidy house. The argument that old reading matter 'might contain some information I need' is often the defence for uncontrolled collecting, while excuses about 'no time to tidy up' often occur in living rooms that don't include enough storage space. Newspapers, magazines and books are space vampires in the living area. Old, yellowing papers piled high in a corner or sprawled in pieces on the sofa are offenders on a number of levels. They are visually unattractive (unless you are an abstract artist working in paper), a potential fire hazard and they steal space. So chaps, gather your loincloths, make the decision to clear the clutter, embark upon the mission and divide things into the Need and Don't Need piles.

Everything in the Need pile should be found a home. Think about building in some alcove shelves and a cupboard if essential items such as CDs and magazines remain homeless. Divide the Need pile into stuff you use every day and stuff you just can't bear to throw away. Much-used items should be found space in an accessible place, others can be stored in the loft, under the stairs or elsewhere.
The Don't Need pile can go in the trash, but preferably recycle items by distributing them to relatives, friends and charity stores.

Crumpled furniture
Sofas that look as if an elephant has spent the night on them then sprawled trampled cushions on the floor during a bad dream, are not appealing. Instead of 'good morning' they say 'bad night.' Abandoned items are not just unsightly, they are also unsanitary and create a 'negative' space.

Keep your sofas and chairs looking smart by plumping up cushions and regular vacuuming. The crumb test – running a small vacuum nozzle, or worse, your own hand down the sides of upholstered furniture is a fast, simple way of weeding out a crop of coins, crumbs and discarded food wrappers that can often cure your furniture of a slightly overused aroma.

Tidy up your seating area by providing magazine racks next to sofas and chairs or buying a low coffee table with a shelf underneath (keep it under control though – no piling up the takeout boxes when no-one's looking).

Clutter bunnies
Clutter bunnies are experts at creating Might Just Need piles. Don't be tempted by this solution unless you have a proven track record for using such things effectively. If in doubt, ask yourself whether you have ever made a delightful papier mâché bowl out of piles of outdated newspapers? Be honest, be ruthless and break the cycle.

File not pile
Cut out any really interesting and useful articles as you read your magazines and put them into a reference file immediately – don't simply create another pile. Mini clutter is as unhelpful as maxi clutter, so store the cuttings in the room in which they will be used. Books that you have finished should be returned to the bookshelf or recycled to a charity book store. Sports kit should find its way to the laundry basket or closet.

Temporary storage
Placing important papers in boxes ready for filing is a form of temporary storage. Collecting together all your photos and storing them in a shoebox in anticipation of arranging them one rainy day in the future, is another useful exercise. Even keeping paperwork and used packaging safely in a designated box for recycling is an effective form of non-permanent storage. If you feel overwhelmed by the idea of de-cluttering all your rooms and putting everything in its final resting place, create some temporary storage and you will feel instantly rewarded.

THE MASS MANTRA

Use this mantra when you are about to tackle the mess:

DOMESTIC
ENERGY
CAN
LIBERATE
U
TOTALLY.
TIDY
EVERY
ROOM

- KEEP A CONTAINER FOR INSTANT TIDY-UPS WHEN YOUR MOTHER VISITS – LOG BASKETS, CRATES ON CASTORS, CARDBOARD STORAGE BOXES CAN ALL BE QUICKLY FILLED AND HIDDEN IN THE SPARE ROOM.
- DON'T ALLOW ANY SPARE SURFACES TO GET PILED UP WITH BELONGINGS. DO A DAILY CHECK AND SCOOP UP ANY PAPERWORK OR CLOTHING THAT BELONGS ELSEWHERE.
- BOYS' TOYS SUCH AS GAMES CONSOLES, EXTRANEOUS HI-FI COMPONENTS AND OTHER SMALL GADGETS AND CABLES CAN BE KEPT IN AN ATTRACTIVE CONTAINER, PREFERABLY BEHIND THE SOFA, AND BROUGHT OUT ONLY WHEN NEEDED.
- TRAIN YOUR PET TO PICK UP LOOSE ITEMS AND DUMP THEM IN THE UTILITY ROOM FOR A SNACK REWARD.

Organizing the chaos

Once you have sorted your belongings into piles and graded them into levels of need, you can start to store. While temporary storage is good for short term items, you should assess your living space and decide where permanently required objects need to go.

Look on storage as a flexible friend. A mixture of freestanding pieces and built-in units is often the answer for housing all those books, magazines and technology. Console games, hi-fis and CDs can quickly look very messy if not contained and concealed, so consult a few magazines or makeover programmes for ideas about which cupboards, drawers, stacking boxes and tables can best answer your needs.

DOMESTIC GOD – STAIRCASE

If you need to take stuff upstairs and don't feel like it, invest in a basket that fits on the stairs smugly. Fill it up in stages. Neat idea?

Dusting

M ost of you reading this will have little idea of just how smart dust is. You probably ignore it or simply pretend it doesn't exist. Warning, warning – you do so at you peril. House dust is very, very smart. It penetrates every crevice, it lives under the sofa, it creeps into your bed, and at the slightest hint of a breeze, it becomes airborne – all the better for invading your orifices and your computer. It will even make a deadly swoop over your food. It is invisible in darkness, it moves silently – it is the enemy. Now is the time to take it seriously, guys. Dust causes allergies, attracts pests and makes the house smell. It has to go.

Dust busting

Regular dusting and vacuuming is absolutely essential. Remember you have to control dust mites, too. These are nasty-looking arachnids that are too small for the naked eye. They live on a high protein diet of skin (yours and your pets, mostly) and other organic matter. Their waste matter (faeces and pulverized bodies) can trigger allergies and are not good for those who suffer from asthma. They are not nice housemates and must be discouraged.

Dust is not only found on flat surfaces at eye level – walls also need dusting and cobwebs need removing regularly. Window frames, blinds and shutters get surprisingly dusty and that tricky-to-access place above the door is another popular spot for homeless particles.

DUSTING TECHNIQUES

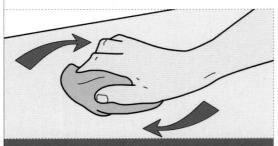

WALL TO WALL OPERATIONS

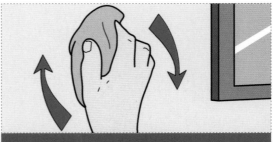

SURFACE TO AIR MISSILES

Dusting is strategic. It's not just a matter of finding an old shirt, ripping it up and flicking it around the odd surface, finishing with a final flourish and a smug grin if doing so before an audience. As with any other exercise, your tools play a very important role. Always use a clean cloth or you will simply transfer the dirt from one surface to the other. If you are dusting walls, use a firm circular motion. Move from top to bottom, left to right (that way you will know which bit you have done).

When dusting delicate surfaces, don't flex your pecs quite as much. A firm but gentle action is the way to go – oval or circular is fine for the motion, but it is a wiping not a flicking movement that you are aiming for. Feather dusters tend to lift dust particles and propel them into the air, rather than gathering and removing them (which is the object of the exercise if you are still wondering). The dust particles will simply float around and settle in a new location. The dust dispersal theory does not work. Invest in some proper cloths and keep them clean. Never, ever use a dirty old sock.

WEAPONS AND TACTICS

There are a few useful ground rules for dust busting. Pay attention to the don'ts as much as the dos:

TOP TO BOTTOM

Think top to bottom, high to low, up to down. There's no point dusting a low-lying table before you dust the walls – the dust will simply spread.

ADHERENCE NOT DISPERSAL

The mission you have undertaken is adherence not dispersal. You want the dust to stick to the cloth not fly around the room at random. If found in possession of a real feather duster, use it with care. It disperses more dust than it deals with.

DUST BEFORE YOU VACUUM

Dust before you vacuum. Unless you enjoy dusting so much you want to do it again.

DRY CLOTH

Use a dry cloth on wooden surfaces and a slightly dampened cloth on others, such as metal or painted surfaces.

COTTON CLOTH

Use a clean, soft cotton cloth or re-use an old (clean) tea towel. Synthetic fibres are not sufficiently absorbent (unless they are special static cloths).

WOOD

Don't get wood damp. Use an impregnated cloth with a dusting aid spray or polish.

CIRCULAR MOTION

Use firm but gentle oval or circular motions. Treat the target with respect. Choose 'lift' rather than 'slide' as a strategy for anything on the surface, such as glass and china ornaments, lamps or knick-knacks of huge sentimental value to you or anyone else.
Mission accomplished. Admire.

Washing and Wiping

R egular dusting and vacuuming of walls and ceilings helps keep them in good condition and makes the 'big spring clean' less daunting, arduous and time-consuming. Use the long brush attachment on your vacuum for the ceiling, applying the principle of top to bottom, high to low (as with dusting on the previous page). Failure to embrace this strategy will result in a temper-testing duplication of the task.

WALL TO WALL

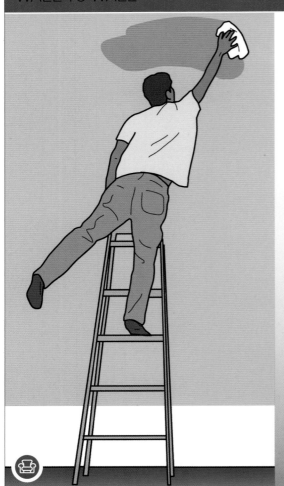

Here's the essential equipment for washing your ceilings and walls:

- A VACUUM CLEANER TO REMOVE DUST FROM CEILING AND WALLS.
- A STRONG AND RELIABLE LADDER OR A HIGH STOOL.
- A BUCKET OF MILD ALL-PURPOSE DETERGENT DILUTED IN WATER (READ THE INSTRUCTIONS FIRST) AND A SECOND BUCKET OF CLEAN WATER.
- A CLEAN CLOTH (OR SPONGE) X 3.
- A PARTNER (EXISTING RATHER THAN POTENTIAL), FRIEND (HELPFUL AND RELIABLE) OR NEIGHBOUR (FRIENDLY NOT VENGEFUL).
- NOT REQUIRED – VERTIGO OR A HANGOVER.

Wall care

Before you start, check that your paintwork is indeed washable. Most painted surfaces are fine, but washing can damage some emulsion paints. Always test-clean a patch (avoiding obvious areas) using diluted detergent and allow to dry. You may decide to repaint surfaces unsuitable for washing.

Wash the ceiling and walls in manageable chunks, using energetic, circular motions, remembering to wring the cloths well at each stage. Always rinse with a clean cloth and dry with another equally pristine one. The top to bottom rule applies here too.

Many wallpapers are washable and the same instructions apply if so, but motions should be more gentle and you must pat the paper dry at the end with a clean, dry cloth. Vacuuming or dusting them first is important and a preliminary test wash of an inconspicuous patch is a good idea, just to be on the safe side.

Up against the wall

Don't forget to remove grubby fingerprints from light switches and their surrounds. Dirty marks on the walls around switches can be removed using a soft eraser.

Remove cobwebs from walls regularly. They are unsightly and you wouldn't want one to land suddenly on top of your partner's mother, would you?

Kitchen walls need washing more frequently than those in other rooms. They are in direct contact with steam, grease and sticky fingers on a daily basis. If your walls are really greasy, wash them down with a solution of sugar soap. It cuts its way through grime and prepares the surface for repainting. Don't be tempted to just paint over dirty walls – it is not the right solution.

If you have wall hangings, give them a good shake from time to time to disturb any moths enjoying free accommodation behind them. Have a wall-washing party – invite a few friends round and tell them it is a BYOB affair (Bring your own Bucket). You provide the beers and the music. It will be done in a flash.

Windows on the world

Dusting or vacuuming your window frames and sills regularly is important for their maintenance. Give the paint a wash every month if you can. Think of your windows as the eyes of your home onto the outside world. Light has to filter through the same obstacles in order to enter the room, affecting both its mood and your own. Dirty windows never make a good impression – it's rather like finding you with a black eye and unwashed on a first encounter. Not the best start you could hope for.

You may want to get a professional to do the outside windows if they are high up or if you suffer from vertigo, but don't try to use these as excuses for failing to tackle the insides. A dull, frost-free day is the best kind for washing windows, as sunlight will dry the windows too rapidly, leaving unwanted streaks. Start by washing the inside frames, then move on to the panes.

The quickest method is to use a commercial window cleaner and a lint-free cloth. A half-and-half solution of vinegar and water is a cheaper substitute, and some people swear by the addition of a few drops of dishwashing liquid. Dry with paper towels or another clean, absorbent, lint-free cloth. For an extra sparkle, finish off with crumpled newspaper. Bet your mother never told you that one.

Blinds and shutters

Dust these with a soft, clean cloth or vacuum with the appropriate dusting attachment. Washing is also necessary from time to time. Venetian or aluminum blinds can all be washed, but paper blinds obviously would not benefit from such treatment. Take the blinds down and wash outside or in the bath, using water and a mild all-purpose cleaner. Rinse and wipe dry. Don't use abrasive substances or ammonia and read the manufacturer's suggested methods of cleaning before you embark on the task. Always rinse with a clean cloth and dry with another equally pristine one. The top to bottom rule applies here, too.

POLISH UP YOUR WAYS

Wood furniture needs regular polishing, and you will probably find that liquids and sprays are the easiest products to use. Take extra care with any antique pieces you may have – wax is the best thing to use on these. Read the instructions on the products carefully before setting about the task, but a few basic techniques generally apply:

- ENSURE THE SURFACE IS DRY AND DUST-FREE.
- USE A SOFT COTTON CLOTH WITH NOTHING ATTACHED THAT COULD SCRATCH THE SURFACE (I.E. NOT AN OLD SHIRT COMPLETE WITH BUTTONS).
- SPREAD POLISH EVENLY OVER THE SURFACE – DIRECTLY OR USING THE CLOTH, DEPENDING ON INSTRUCTIONS.
- BUFF WITH A SECOND CLEAN CLOTH.
- ADMIRE HIGHLY POLISHED REFLECTION (OF SELF).

Stain Removal

Stains are inevitable within the home, however much care you may take to prevent them, but the quicker you act, the more successful you are likely to be at removing them.

STAIN BUSTERS
Walls and paintwork
Unwanted scribbling on the walls calls for bicarbonate of soda diluted with a little water in a small bowl to form a thick paste. Rub gently on the offending mark.

Stain removal on wallpaper is a tricky business and you may end up making things worse. Choose from a wide selection of commercial substances, including solvents, but follow instructions carefully and check they are safe for your type of wallpaper. Sometimes, rubbing dirty patches with stale white bread has been known to work (who said household management was predictable?).

Carpets
For carpet spillages, time is of the essence. If you allow a carpet stain to set, you will have a very hard job removing it. Think stain, think SBS – scoop, blot, solution. Act swiftly and scoop up as much of the solid or semi-solid spill as you can, using a spoon or spatula, if necessary.

Remove all excess wet material by blotting with a paper towel or soft cloth. Apply small amounts of a detergent solution (a quarter of a teaspoon of mild, clear liquid detergent mixed with a cup of lukewarm water) using a cloth or paper towel. Start at the outside and gradually blot towards the centre. Repeat the whole process with plain lukewarm water.

Upholstery
Many of the principles applied to removing stains from carpets apply to upholstery. Always do a pre-test with the selected solution (see opposite) on a part of the fabric that will not show, having read the care instructions on the label. Some fabrics will fade and therefore should not be washed.

Floors
Before you set about removing stains from wood flooring, it is important to ascertain if the stain or scratch is in the wood itself or on the topcoat finish.

Natural- or Wax-finish Floors / Floors Without Hard Finishes
You can repair scratches with wax (more about that on page 71) but food stains require a little more brain and brawn. Gently rub the stain with a damp cloth, rub dry and then wax. Again, the working from outside in principle applies. Water stains should be rubbed with steel wool and then waxed. White rings can be removed using a paste of salt and olive oil left on the stain overnight. Wipe off the next morning and re-wax.

Wood Floors with Hard Finishes or Varnishes, including Polyurethane
Care needs to be taken with such floors (you can detect them by checking to see if the stain is in the superficial finish). Scratches should be repaired with specialist kits available from flooring retailers and other stains should be treated with specialist cleaners for urethane finishes.

STAIN REMOVAL KIT

Every household needs a stain removal kit primed for action at any moment. For general household incidents, the following equipment is all you need. Make up your own kit by photocopying the list and taking it to a large supermarket or hardware store to source everything:

- ABSORBENT PAPER TOWELS OR SPONGES
- CLEAN, ABSORBENT WHITE CLOTHS
- ALL-PURPOSE DETERGENT
- WHITE VINEGAR
- WHITE SPIRIT
- BLEACH
- AMMONIA
- NON-OILY NAIL VARNISH REMOVER (BUY-IN SPECIALLY, IT'S WORTH IT)
- LAUNDRY STAIN PRE-TREATMENT PRODUCT

- SPECIALIST STAIN REMOVERS (FOR THINGS LIKE BALLPOINT OR FELT-TIP STAINS)
- RUBBING ALCOHOL
- BICARBONATE OF SODA
- SOLVENT-TYPE CLEANING FLUIDS OR DRY-CLEANING FLUIDS
- NON-SOLVENT STAIN OR SPOT REMOVER
- LEMONS

REMOVING A STAIN

1 Don't waste time. Grab some paper towel and act. Pulling a rug over the stain won't help. Ignoring it won't make it go away. It's like toothache. Think SBS – scoop, blot, solution. If it's a liquid spill, it's more of a BBS – blot, blot solution technique. Blot with paper towel or a soft, clean and colourfast cloth. Work from the outside in – if the spill looks like a map of Europe, don't transform it into a map of the entire world.

2 If the spill is solid or semi-solid, you need to scoop up as much of it as you can with a spoon, spatula or similar blunt object. Don't use a carving knife – cutting out a stain is not a solution. Be careful to contain the spill. Don't play with it or push it around aimlessly. This is serious stuff and you need to get a grip. Don't rub the spill into the carpet. The mission is to lift and separate it from the accident zone.

3 Now is the time to apply the cleaning substance. Use a mixture of detergent and water (see page 48) or a specialist commercial stain remover. Read the instructions before application. It's a good idea to do a test patch first in an inconspicuous spot. Apply the cleaning substance directly to the stain, give it time to do its work and then blot clean with more paper towel or a clean, soft colourfast cloth. Blot from the outside in.

4 You might need to repeat this process to remove all evidence of the spill. The final tactic is to spray plain, lukewarm water over the offending area and blot as usual. Once the carpet is dry, gently brush or vacuum the area to restore its pile and glory. If you fancy steam- or dry-cleaning your carpets, call in the professionals. It's quite an operation and should be undertaken only by the very confident! Keep your carpets looking good by regular vacuuming.

FABRIC STAIN BUSTERS

Different stains need different solutions. Here are a few of the more common substances you may find yourself dealing with:

ALCOHOL: BEER AND WINE (AND SOY SAUCE!)
a) Mix one teaspoon of mild detergent with a cup of lukewarm water and blot.
b) Mix 80ml of white vinegar with 160ml of water and blot.
c) Sponge with clean water and blot. (for wine it is advisable to repeat step a)

CHOCOLATE, COFFEE AND TEA
a) Again, mix one teaspoon of mild detergent with a cup of lukewarm water and blot.
b) Mix 80ml of white vinegar this time with120ml of water and blot.
c) Sponge with clean water and blot.

CURRY
Curry is one of the most difficult and stubborn stains to remove. It's a delicious takeout but an almost impossible get-out. Time to bring in the professionals – dry cleaning is the best solution (literally).

The Fireplace

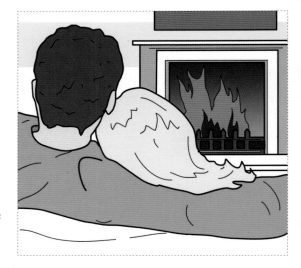

I f the kitchen is the HQ of the household, the brains of the organism (see pages 12–37), then the fireplace is the heart and the belly, responsible for radiating warmth and comfort, if not literally then certainly symbolically. Ever since Homo Erectus discovered fire 400,000 years ago, the hearth has been an important focal point for friends and families to gather, a glass of wine or a cup of tea in hand.

Ashes to ashes

Removing the ashes is not a dead end job. Just think of all the fun Cinderella had at the ball and the way her career opened up. She will have been well aware of the need to ensure that the ashes are completely extinguished before removal. You should wait 24-48 hours and take care – hot embers are clever at camouflage and may lurk concealed in the ash. The Cinderella Kit includes:

- A FIREPROOF CONTAINER WITH A HANDLE (E.G. A METAL BUCKET OR RUBBISH BIN)
- A SMALL SHOVEL
- A DUSTPAN AND BRUSH

Gather the ashes with a shovel and gently empty into the metal container. Brush the grate and hearth. Once the dust has settled, wipe the front area of the hearth with a damp floor cloth. Store the ashes outside in a metal rubbish bin with a tight lid. Gardeners will be interested to know that wood ash can be spread on the compost heap but coal fire ash cannot.

Chimney care

It is extremely important to have your chimney inspected and cleaned. Regularly used chimneys should be checked and swept annually, bi-annually or quarterly, depending on the type of fuel you use. Otherwise the build-up of soot can cause a chimney fire and dangerous gases can also accumulate inside the home. Chimney fires are pretty frightening – don't even think about running the risk of one just to save money. A chimney sweep will remove creosote, birds' nests or other debris and blockages.

The fire surround

If your fire surround is made of painted wood or tiles, a regular wipe down with a damp cloth and a monthly wash with soapy water should suffice. Cast-iron fire surrounds need a thorough clean to remove all the dirt and grease, followed by the occasional spray of specialist matt black paint (for fireplaces and wood-burning stoves). Wipe slate with a damp cloth and for an extra sheen, wipe with a clean cloth soaked in linseed oil. Marble is a delicate surface and needs to be treated with care. Microcrystalline wax will protect it from smoke and stains. If your home has an antique fireplace, it's probably best to call in the professionals.

Wood-burning stoves

These are generally more efficient at heating a room than the conventional open fireplace. A large percentage of the heat generated by a stove actually warms the room. Your chimney must have a lined flue if you intend to have a wood-burning stove – always call in the professionals to install it. If you burn wood, remove the ash regularly but leave a bed about 2.5 cm (1 in) thick. If you burn coal, remove the ash daily. Fire up the stove at least once a day rather than leave it damped down all the time. The flue should be swept annually or bi-annually.

Electric fireplaces

If you want all the special effects but none of the hassle, buy an electric fire complete with realistic-looking flames and the sound of real crackling logs. All you need to do is switch it on (the fire and the charm that is).

Smoke detectors

Smoke detectors save lives. Make sure you know and follow any specific regulations for your area or type of building, but in general you should have one on every floor of your home, including the basement. Always put one in any room with a heater and be sure to put one in your garage and workshop. Kitchens and bathrooms are generally not recommended as locations for smoke detectors, since steam can trigger them, but bedrooms and hallways are important locations, as is the top of each staircase. Follow the manufacturer's instructions for placing, checking, testing and maintaining your smoke detectors.

Carbon monoxide detectors

You can't see it, you can't smell it, but carbon monoxide gas is poisonous. It is present in car and lawn mower exhaust fumes and can come from chimneys, wood or gas stoves, oil and gas boilers, gas water heaters, gas dryers, gas or paraffin portable heaters. Make sure you have your fuel-burning appliances inspected by a trained professional at the beginning of each heating season. Carbon monoxide detectors are recommended by all the safety experts. Like smoke alarms, they emit a loud shriek when triggered and should be installed on each level of your home, including in or just outside your bedroom. Remember, they are not smoke alarms and do not detect smoke or fire.

STAY SAFE

- DON'T LEAVE THE ROOM WITHOUT PUTTING UP THE FIREGUARD OR SCREEN.
- DON'T GO TO BED UNTIL A FIRE HAS BURNT ITSELF OUT.
- DON'T LEAVE CHILDREN OR PETS UNATTENDED IN A ROOM IN WHICH A FIRE IS BURNING.
- DON'T LEAVE THE AREA AROUND THE FIREPLACE WITH CLUTTER THAT COULD EASILY IGNITE, SUCH AS MAGAZINES, NEWSPAPERS, PIZZA BOXES OR TOYS.
- NEVER LEAVE A LIT CANDLE UNATTENDED.
- NEVER LEAVE CANDLES BURNING WHEN YOU GO TO BED.
- KEEP MATCHES AND LIGHTERS STORED OUT OF THE REACH OF CHILDREN.
- KEEP SPARE LOGS WELL AWAY FROM THE FIRE – SPARKS ARE GOOD AT LONG JUMPING.
- DON'T BURN WRAPPING PAPER IN A FIREPLACE – IT COULD START A CHIMNEY FIRE.
- DON'T SPRAY AEROSOLS NEAR TO AN OPEN FLAME.
- PLACE A FEW PIECES OF ORANGE PEEL AMONG THE KINDLING FOR A FRAGRANT FIRE.

LAYING A FIRE IN AN OPEN FIREPLACE

Every self-respecting 21st-century Homo Erectus will need all or some of the following:

- PAPER – SCRUNCHED INTO TIGHT BALLS OF NEWSPAPER, NOT CASUALLY STREWN IN LIMP SHEETS.
- KINDLING STICKS – VERY DRY TWIGS OR WOOD.
- FIRELIGHTERS – FOR THE NOVICE OR THE IMPATIENT (YOU CAN ALWAYS HIDE THE PACKAGING) AND MATCHES.
- COAL (WHERE ALLOWED) OR SMOKELESS FUEL – GIVES YOU THE IMPORTANT EMBERS AND THE INTRINSIC, LONG-TERM WARMTH.
- WELL-SEASONED HARDWOOD LOGS.

Ensure the room is well ventilated. Lay the newspaper and firelighters in the centre of the clean grate and stack the kindling around it, leaving plenty of air spaces. Light the paper and once the kindling is burning, gradually add the main fuel (logs and/or coal). The harder the wood you use, the longer and hotter the fire will burn. Some fires burn well if the ashes are regularly cleared and others are better if you leave a bed of ashes in place under the grate. You will soon get to know the little idiosyncrasies of your own fireplace and become its master, if not its friend.

Caring for Fabrics and Textiles

I n your living room, when you have finally chosen your curtains, blinds and furniture then restyled the space – be it bachelor pad, love shack, homely nest or technology lab – you will have to care for its contents in just the same way as you do your wardrobe.

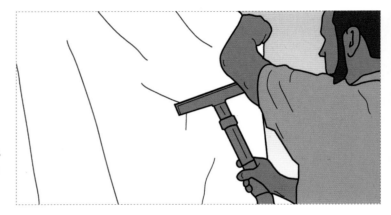

Curtains and blinds

The good news is that you will need to wash or professionally clean your curtains far less often if you remove dust and cobwebs regularly with the appropriate upholstery nozzle on your vacuum cleaner, always remembering to put it on low suction, of course. The strategy is a top to bottom, high to low one for curtains, using short, repeated strokes. If your curtains have heavy trimmings or fringing, a good tip is to cover the head of the nozzle or brush with a piece of net curtain. Vacuum curtains in bedrooms once a week and in other areas once a month if you can. It is not too time consuming and saves effort and money in the end, as with so many other household tasks. If dirt and dust build up in the fabric they can cause premature weakening or fading of even the most colourfast fabrics.

How to avoid curtains for your curtains

The frequency with which curtains need washing or cleaning will depend largely on just how clean the air is in and around your home. Curtains that contend with open fires, cigarette smoke and high levels of environmental air pollution on a regular basis will mean more frequent cleaning.

When deciding whether to wash or dry-clean your curtains and draperies, read the care labels first. A good maxim is 'if in doubt, leave 'em out and send 'em out'. Well-intentioned removal of your window dressings followed by enthusiastic jettison into the washing machine could mean curtains for your curtains. Many curtains are simply not washable so bear this in mind. Shrinking or discoloration can occur, together with all sorts of other damage that might not immediately spring to mind (e.g. flame-retardant treatments could be seriously reduced through machine washing).

If you do wash your curtains in the machine, here are a few tips:

- REMOVE ALL CURTAIN HOOKS AND LOOSEN ANY TAPE DRAW STRINGS.
- CHOOSE A GENTLE CYCLE WITH LUKEWARM OR COOL WATER.
- OPT FOR A LIQUID DETERGENT THAT DOES NOT CONTAIN BLEACHING OR OPTICAL BRIGHTENING AGENTS.
- DO NOT OVERLOAD THE MACHINE.
- TUMBLE DRY ON LOW TO AVOID SHRINKAGE (OR LINE DRY).
- IRON WHILE DAMP (LENGTHWISE AND ON THE REVERSE ONLY) (MORE ABOUT IRONING ON PAGE 50.)

Upholstery

You get upholstery vacuuming under your belt on page 75 – now it's time to check out the art and craft of upholstery shampooing. Don't panic, you will only need to do it every year or two, unless you have a very large family or a collection of tame wildebeest as house guests. You can call in the professionals or do the job yourself with a home steam extraction machine (purchased or hired). If you go for the DIY option, read the manufacturer's instructions very carefully, test patch an inconspicuous area and make sure the newly-cleaned fabric dries as quickly as possible. You can also hand-shampoo upholstery using a commercial upholstery cleaner. Spray onto the fabric, rub vigorously and then vacuum. You must ensure you read the instructions carefully and that the shampoo is safe for your particular fabric. Inappropriate cleaning can reduce the fire safety of the fabric.

Care or cure: sofas so good

Sofas need frequent vacuuming, so get used to it. Anyway, more vacuuming needs less shampooing, so think yourself lucky. Vacuum regularly, use throws, slipcovers and waterproofing or soil-repellent sprays (always bearing in mind fire safety precautions), and try to prevent marauding animals, children and disorderly guests from using your sofa as a playpen, trampoline or temporary home, while sporting dirty paws, muddied boots or belts with buckles. Direct sunlight will cause the fabric to fade and should be avoided where possible. Tip of the day: throws stay in place better with patches of Velcro sewn on the reverse.

Lounge lizard leather

Leather-clad furniture or desktops do not require much maintenance. A quick dust followed by a gentle rub with saddle soap and a chance to dry completely, and the sofa is ready for a spot of horizontal posing once more.

Lampshades

Lampshades don't fit in washing machines so you must try and dust them with both care and regularity. You can vacuum on low suction with the appropriate dust brush in one hand and a firm grip on the shade with the other. Plastic shades can be wiped with a damp cloth, but don't wet paper shades. If you are feeling brave, you can immerse a washable fabric lampshade in a washing solution, checking first that it will not emerge a different shape, colour or item. Antique or particularly delicate shades should be treated with extreme care. A gentle brush or vacuum using a 'softly softly' technique is all that should be undertaken without consulting an expert.

Horizontal hygiene

If you have a sofa-bed, make sure you relieve it of its horizontal status as soon as possible the next morning, particularly if it is in the main living area. Make sure you wash the sheets and mattress cover regularly. Just because someone spent only one night on it doesn't mean you only launder the linen once a year. If guests arrive with their own bedlinen, you will know you have work to do on that score. A good way of saving on the washing front is to ask your guests if they mind sleeping inside a duvet or doona cover – it makes a great one-piece top and bottom sheet alternative. It works better for single guests – two people trapped inside one cover can be rather more 'sardine' than 'snug'.

Launder or dry clean sofa throws and removable cushion covers at least every season (check if they are safe to put in the washing machine before you press the 'On' button). The good thing about throws is that you can replace them quite cheaply – ring the changes, buy a new one for spring.

GOOD SOFA, BAD SOFA

Sofas and couches reflect their owner's personality. Look at yours. Is it neat, tidy, in good condition, all plumped up, welcoming and ready to offer comfort or support? Does it invite you to relax, enjoy a quiet moment of contemplation or a good book? Or is it a mess, covered in food and drink stains, unapproachable and frankly rather unappealing? Do you think guests want to jump up and down on it, chuck it out, give it a wash or sink between its arms? There are good and bad people around. There are good and bad sofas in the world, too. Here's how to tell them apart.

Good sofa	Bad sofa
A good sofa is one that commands respect and is in the right place at the right time. It is not in direct sunlight, its cushions are all present and correct, all fluffed up and ready to do their job (when plumping cushions, work from the sides, by the way). It is clean, dust-free and orderly. It is not a refuge for lost belongings. It doesn't look like an elephant slept on it or a gymnast used it to perfect a triple somersault. If it could speak, and sofas do say volumes about you, it would exclaim 'hello and welcome, do take a seat.'	A bad sofa is a paradise for four-legged creatures, an exercise zone for small two-legged ones and a semi-permanent home for sofa slobs. It has nasty marks and tears. Clouds of dust emerge when you sit on it. Pizza boxes lurk beneath the cushions and socks hide in singles under the base. It has never met a vacuum cleaner. It is a stranger to shampoo. It grunts 'beware, don't approach, you might meet something unpleasant.' Don't be a sofa slob or a couch potato. Take control and give your sofa its role and soul back. Take action and you might see some.

Floors without Flaws

R egular vacuuming preserves both your carpet's quality and appearance (see page 72) but why not try to minimize dirt in the first place? Use a dirt-trapping doormat at the front door or entrance to the room and rugs or runners in the hallway. Establish a rule that people wipe shoes and boots at the front door and try adopting the Japanese tradition of removing footwear before entering the home.

Move the furniture periodically (lift not push please) to avoid permanent crushing. Use castors and protectors under furniture legs to prevent squashing the pile. A handy hint that really works for removing dents is to place an ice cube in each one. As the cube melts the fibres swell. Run over the dents with a vacuum cleaner and the wet fibres will become upright again. Neat, eh?

Natural is nice
Many people opt for natural floor coverings such as sisal, jute or coir nowadays. They are hardwearing alternatives and work well in households with small two-legged or four-legged inhabitants. They should be vacuumed regularly (the floors, not the children or pets) and on both sides if they are rugs. Stains are less obvious on such floorings but that doesn't mean you can leave them. To remove mud or other solids, lift off the excess with care and leave the rest to dry. Brush along the weave with a stiff brush and then vacuum. Liquid spills should be dealt with swiftly. Blot firmly, working from the outside in. Avoid wetting the area further and don't even think of using a conventional carpet shampoo. For persistent stains, call in the professionals.

LIFT, DON'T SLIDE

When dusting, you should always apply the 'lift, don't slide' principle. It's the same with chairs and other furniture on the floor. Don't drag chairs from one place to the next. It makes an unpleasant noise and leaves marks, creating bad impressions on a number of levels.

Floor etiquette
Don't drag chairs noisily to the table when entertaining guests. Lift and separate from the floor to prevent hospitality headaches.

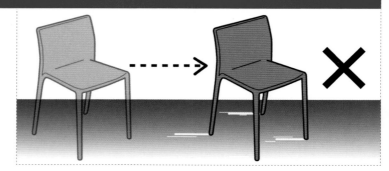

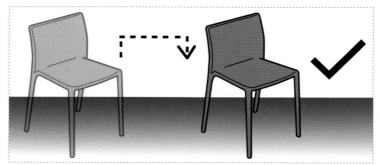

SOLID HARDWOOD FLOORS

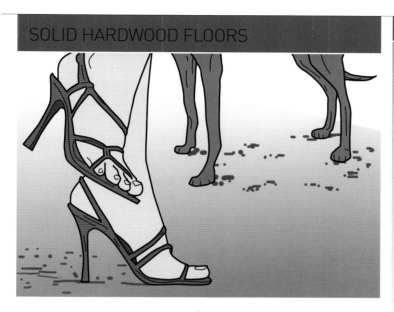

OTHER FLOORS

Cork floors
If you have a cork floor, take extra care. Vacuum or sweep regularly but resist the temptation to rush off and get the mop and bucket. Remember, cork floors are made from the cork tree and are therefore organic. They need to be cleaned with appropriate specialist liquids and waxes. Ask your local hardware store to advise you. Always deal with spills as soon as they occur. You may well prevent the formation of stains by so doing. Act now, no need to repent later.

Linoleum floors
Linoleum is becoming increasingly popular. Made with linseed oil, ground cork, wood, flour and resins, it is quite environmentally sound while being comfortable and warm. Amazingly enough, it is also able to destroy bacteria on the floor naturally, leaving you with less work. Cleaning is easy. Just sweep and vacuum thoroughly (but not aggressively) before washing with detergent and warm water. Always lift furniture and heavy items to avoid making marks and dents. Protect the floor from very heavy items with furniture protector pads available from most hardware stores. Self-adhesive protective pads are a good idea for heavy furniture on most floors.

Rugs
Rugs are a great idea for the living area. They can introduce colour to the room while protecting the floor from heavy traffic. Anchoring a rug to the floor using a non-slip felt mat equipped with an adhesive base will keep it safely in place. Rugs don't escape attack by nasty critters and need to be vacuumed regularly.

Dirt, grit and sand:
will scratch, dent and dull your floors. Invest in floor mats and keep floors clean. Sweep regularly using a broom equipped with fine ends that can trap the dirt effectively.

Pets:
with long nails and weak bladders scratch and stain wood. Train your pets and trim their claws (sadly, felt pads don't work on dogs and cats).

Liquid spills:
(water, coffee, wine etc.) left for any length of time on the floor will cause stains. Wipe up spills as soon as they happen.

Ladies:
with high heels and dangerous stilettos can leave an impression on you and your floor. Ask them politely to remove their perilous footwear – everyone will feel more comfortable.

Furniture:
dragged across the floor will cause dents and scratches – lift your furniture and put felt pads under the legs of chairs and tables. Dragging went out with the cavemen.

Shoes:
with damaged heels equal potential damage. Repair your shoes regularly and check your partner and house-mates do the same. Guests are harder to boss around.

Chewing gum:
and wax deposits don't belong on your floor. Put ice on them until the deposit becomes brittle and crumbles off with careful assistance from you and a knife.

Direct sunlight:
can discolour the wood. Keep blinds and curtains closed to protect from strong and direct sunlight.

Vacuuming

There are a few important things you need to know about vacuuming. First of all, it is not too time-consuming, particularly if you do it regularly. Vacuuming is not a chore – it is a quick way of making the place and indeed you yourself feel better (really, it is). You can save money by vacuuming – it prolongs the life of your carpet by preventing dust and dirt from settling deep into the fibres and damaging them. In an ideal world you would vacuum every day, but if you just don't have time, focus on the heavy traffic zones and vacuum a couple of times in between the weekly vacuuming. Think of how you are burning calories and building muscle.

Even bare floors benefit from vacuuming along the grain. Your machine will probably have attachments for specific uses, surfaces and degrees of suction. Read the instructions carefully. As a general rule, think the harder or denser the target fabric, the stronger the suction required.

A clean sweep
For sweeping, a sturdy broom is an effective tool for removing large particles on floors that see lots of action, such as living areas, kitchens, hallways, utility rooms and porches. Use the outside – in principle, again, to avoid aimlessly pushing the dust back into the air. Your aim is to collect the dirt in the centre of the room.

Size does matter and small is useful
A smaller brush can be very handy for sweeping the dirt into the dustpan or getting into tight corners or nooks and crannies. Brush as much dirt as you can into the dustpan and then move it back a little to scoop up the dirt you missed the first time.

LOW PEC HI TECH

New technology does happen in the cleaning world too. You can now buy special long-handled devices that have removable, replaceable static cloths on the end. They allow you to swish around uncarpeted floors with speed and grace, collecting dust through a static process. It's quick, easy, effective – and more than a little stylish.

BEFORE

AFTER

SWEEPING TACTICS

There's more to sweeping than meets the eye. To avoid dust meeting the eye you need a sweeping strategy (and it's not under the carpet). Identify the target, the tactics and the tools.

Target: dust and debris. Tactic: collect and clear. Tools: broom and brush. Imagine the room as a circle and the focus of your mission its centre. Use firm, focussed strokes to sweep the dirt towards target.

Once collated, use a small dustpan and brush to collect the collateral damage. A second strike will mean mission accomplished.

The big brush off

Sweeping the carpets is not generally necessary or useful, although you might want to collect stubborn pet hair with a small brush. If you have wooden floors in your living area, it's a different matter. You can sweep, dust or vacuum those. If you are an all-in-one kind of guy, there are products out there that profess to be the ultimate in multi-tasking, multi-purpose cleaners with mop heads, built-in wringers, detachable broom heads with powers to generate enough static electricity to lift pet hair from carpets and hard floors. And they can be used outdoors to scrub yards, paths and patios. They are the equivalent of the guy who's good at science, art, technology, romance and housework – a sort of 21st-century Leonardo da Vinci with a plug.

FOUR FACTS ABOUT VACUUMING

- JUST THIRTY MINUTES OF STRENUOUS DIRT-BUSTING WILL BURN AROUND 100 CALORIES.

- FOR SOME PEOPLE, VACUUMING RELEASES FEEL-GOOD HORMONES. FOR OTHERS IT HAS A MORE NEGATIVE IMPACT. IF YOU DON'T MIND IT AND YOUR PARTNER DISLIKES IT INTENSELY, OFFER TO DO MORE THAN YOUR SHARE. EARN SOME REWARD POINTS. YOU MIGHT WIN A PRIZE.

- OVER 70 PER CENT OF PEOPLE FORGET TO VACUUM THE EDGES OF CARPETS AND THE SKIRTING BOARDS. YOU CAN CHANGE THIS STATISTIC. DUST BUNNIES THRIVE IN HIDDEN, NEGLECTED SPOTS. ZAP THEM BEFORE THEY ZAP YOU.

- IF YOUR MOTHER OR BOSS CALLS UP UNEXPECTEDLY TO SAY THEY ARE ON THEIR WAY, VACUUM THE HALLWAY AND OBVIOUS PARTS OF THE LIVING AREA. SPRAY FURNITURE POLISH IN THE AIR AND SOME GENTLE AIR FRESHENER IN THE BATHROOM. POLISH THE TAPS. THIS SHOULD DIVERT ATTENTION AWAY FROM DETAIL.

The Vacuum Cleaner

V acuum cleaners are fabulous things. Every part and component is devoted to keeping your home cleaner and more hygienic than any other machine you are likely to have. Vacuuming is a two-way street. You need to flex your muscles, too. OK, vacuums cleaners aren't as sleek and glamorous as a sports car, but they can give you a smooth ride and have room for speed stripes down the side. Add a spoiler, put on your sunglasses, turn up the sound and get into top gear. It's like driving a convertible indoors. If your machine is wheezing, coughing and belching out dust, it's time to think seriously about trading it in. Ask the retailer to advise on the best model for your particular needs. You may have more polished floors than carpets, several sets of stairs or none at all. There's a model to suit every domestic context.

1 Dust bag: Most of the dust becomes trapped inside while air escapes through pores in the bag.

2 Filtering system: Residual dust is removed from the air by the filtering system.

3 Expelled air

4 Fan: The rotating fan expels clean air, creating a partial vacuum inside the dust bag.

5 Rotating Brush: The rotating brush loosens dirt from carpets and rugs.

The first portable vacuum cleaner to be powered by an electric motor was introduced in 1907. The British inventor James Dyson came up with the bag-less machine in the early 1990s, making a major breakthrough in home cleaning with his dual cyclone system. His invention replaced the traditional porous bag with two cyclone chambers that spin the air to extract dust from it. There are lots of different vacuum designs to choose from, including uprights, canisters, bagless, cordless, large and small. You just need to decide which works best in your home.

Conventional upright and canister vacuum cleaners use a fan to create a partial vacuum and suck dirty air from carpets, rugs, upholstery and bare floors through a paper or cloth bag. Air passes through the microscopic pores of the bag but dust is left behind, which can be disposed of later. Dyson's cyclone uses a spinning column of air instead of a bag to extract the dust. It spins dirty air rapidly inside a drum, forcing dust outward to the wall, just as water is forced out of a spin dryer. The dust, separated from the air, collects in a plastic container.

Upright vacuum cleaner
The electric motor of an upright vacuum cleaner spins a fan at up to 300 revolutions per second, expelling air from the back of the machine. This creates a partial vacuum inside the machine, which causes dirt and air to be sucked up through the bottom of the machine into a dust bag. Most of the dust becomes trapped inside, while the clean air passes through the bag's pores and is drawn through a filter system.

KNOW YOUR ATTACHMENTS

When becoming intimate with a vacuum cleaner, you will have to meet its various attachments. It's rather like the early stages of a new relationship. It's important to know who is who and who does what. Alternatively, think of each attachment as an aspect of your own personality; each one is effective in a particular environment.

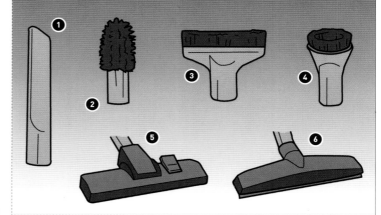

1. Crevice brush
Seek and destroy. Gets into crevices and cracks you didn't know you had.

2. Radiator nozzle
Good at cleaning radiators, strangely enough.

3. Upholstery nozzle
Good at vacuuming sofas, cushions, curtains, mattresses and other furnishings.

4. Dusting Brush
Tackles dust on all sorts of surfaces, whatever shape (due to a 360° swivel action).

5. Combination Floor Tool
Equipped with versatile, straight suction for smooth or carpeted surfaces and delicate rugs

6. Smooth floor brush
Bit of a smooth operator. Focuses on floors such as parquet, stone or vinyl

HANDY HELP

Cordless handheld or upright vacuums are extremely useful additions to your household equipment. They are great at zapping crumbs and dirt with minimum effort and maximum speed. Perfect for panic clean-ups when your mother calls unexpectedly to say she is on her way.

DINING ROOM

Plant Life
Choose plants that suit the conditions of the room.

Polish Up
Dust and polish surfaces every week. Use flower arrangements to improve the ambience.

Be Prepared
Impromptu dinner parties go more smoothly if your room is prepared. Protect your dining table with mats or a cloth.

'THE LAST THING A SMART MAN NEEDS
IN THE DINING ROOM IS A DUMB WAITER.'

Robert Swift

Declutter
Keep the dining area free of clutter
and old computers. Vacuum the
floor before and after meals.

Dining Room

I f you don't have a separate dining room at home, don't worry. These days areas of the kitchen or living room are often used for more formal or special occasion meals with friends, partners or family. Indeed, gathering around a table to enjoy a meal in a relaxed and welcoming atmosphere is one of life's great pleasures.

All you need is a generous-sized table, a number of chairs and enough space for placing dishes, bottles and other dining accessories. Keep the area free of clutter that may have gravitated here from other rooms.

Excessive heat or cold may distract attention from the food, and will do little to create a relaxed atmosphere. If guests arrive wearing thick coats and are noticeably unwilling to take them off or, conversely, turn up in beach attire on a winter's day, you know you have to work on the ambience.

CHORE CHART: WHAT TO DO WHEN

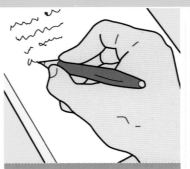

DAILY:
- CLEAR CLUTTER
- TIDY AND CLEAN SURFACES

WEEKLY:
- VACUUM OR SCRUB FLOORS
- PLAN FOR ANY GATHERINGS

MONTHLY:
- WASH WINDOWS
- DUST BLINDS
- CLEAN AND TIDY CUPBOARDS AND DRAWERS

X NO-NOS

Mess attracts mess and clutter never creates a soothing atmosphere, so here's how to manage your entertaining zone:

1. HATS (AND PHONES) OFF

Don't forget to relieve your guests of their coats, hats and baggage at the front door and put them in the bedroom or hallway. They won't feel relaxed if their outdoor wear takes up as much room as they do on the chair, signalling that they are not expected to stay long. Take their phones away too to make sure they relax (unless they have very small children and babysitters at home of course).

2. ANY OLD IRON

Don't use your dining room as a repository for old or underused equipment that you haven't quite got round to removing or selling. It is all too easy for a little-used room to become the equivalent of an overloaded filing tray marked 'down but not yet out', littered with stuff that you no longer use on a regular basis but whose future is as yet undetermined.

3. SMILES NOT PILES

If you use your dining table for studying, working, doing jigsaws or pursuing other hobbies, don't leave the tools of your trade lying around as clutter. Hurriedly hiding piles of belongings under the sofa at the last minute before guests arrive is not a solution you should get used to. Keep the area tidy even when you don't have plans to entertain.

4. DON'T TAKE IT AWAY, MAESTRO

You were feeling sociable, you asked a few friends round for dinner, they said yes – now what do you do? Panic? No need. Try to avoid the easy option of a takeout served in its box or container and ice cream passed round in its tub. Instead, reward your guests for making the effort to come to your house, armed with a nice bottle of wine. Plan to spoil them with food you have prepared yourself.

Table Preparation

I t is worth making the effort to decorate the table when you entertain. Your guests will enjoy the occasion much more and are bound to admire your presentation skills even before you dazzle them with your culinary ones.

You should aim to spoil your guests, not your table, so always use a tablecloth to protect it and the dishes, and also to muffle the sound of glasses and plates hitting the table (intentionally or accidentally). Choose fabric rather than plastic for the tablecloth and (ironed) cloth rather than paper napkins. Don't clutter the surface with lots of jars, cartons or tubs of butter. It's not a good look.

Who sits where

Try to have an idea of a seating plan, if only to avoid awkwardness when people approach the table, unsure of where to place themselves. If you have an equal mix of male and female guests, try the girl, boy, girl, boy strategy, persuading couples not to sit next to each other if possible, unless the romance is a very new one. Strictly speaking, a newcomer to the group should sit to the right of the host in order to be given due attention. If you have guests who have political views that are at opposite ends of the spectrum from one another and want to keep the evening light-hearted, you may want to direct them to opposite ends of the table. If you have a no-show, remove the relevant place setting and chair, encourage those to the left and right of the missing person to huddle closer together. This will keep the atmosphere, if not your seating plan, intact. Try and sit yourself within easy reach of the kitchen and don't let a guest sit at the end of the table with an empty space next to them.

LAYING THE TABLE

It may come as a surprise to some that there are a number of different ways to lay the table, depending on the timing of the occasion and its level of formality. For the purposes of a dinner party with friends, you may find it helpful to digest some or all of the following:

- CUTLERY AND GLASSES SHOULD BE CLEAN (SPARKLINGLY SO, IF POSSIBLE) AND MATCHING.
- KNIVES AND SPOONS SHOULD BE PLACED TO THE RIGHT OF THE PLATE AND FORKS TO THE LEFT.
- KNIFE EDGES POINT INWARDS—BLADES TOWARDS THE PLATE.
- THE CUTLERY APPEARS IN THE ORDER IN WHICH IT WILL BE USED, WORKING FROM THE OUTSIDE IN.
- NAPKINS SHOULD BE PLACED TO THE LEFT OF THE FORK.
- GLASSES SHOULD BE PLACED AT THE TOP RIGHT EDGE OF THE PLATE, NEAR THE TIP OF THE KNIFE, WITH THE WINE GLASS TO THE RIGHT OF THE WATER GLASS.
- DESSERT UTENSILS CAN START OFF ABOVE THE PLATE AND THEN BE PLACED ON EITHER SIDE OF THE DESSERT PLATE AFTER YOU HAVE CLEARED AWAY AT THE END OF THE MEAL.
- SALT AND PEPPER SHOULD BE WITHIN EVERYONE'S REACH—YOU MAY NEED A COUPLE OF SETS IF YOU ARE ENTERTAINING MORE THAN, SAY, SIX PEOPLE.
- PLACE CONDIMENTS, SAUCES AND BUTTER IN SMALL DISHES WITH IMPLEMENTS (YES, EVEN THE KETCHUP).

LAYING THE TABLE

When serving a meal, this is the usual order in which to present each course:

- HORS D'OEUVRE
- SOUP OR PASTA
- MAIN COURSE (E.G. FISH, MEAT, PASTA)
  WITH SALAD OR SALAD TO FOLLOW
- CHEESE
- DESSERT (OR DESSERT FOLLOWED BY CHEESE)
- COFFEE OR TEA

Naturally, you don't have to serve all of the above courses. However, do ensure your guests don't go hungry. Too much food is far better than too little. If you find guests secretly dialling the pizza delivery number as they leave the house, you will know you got the quantities wrong. Leftovers are tomorrow's lunch.

KNOW YOUR PLACE

NAPKIN   BREAD PLATE   SALAD PLATE   DINNER PLATE   WATER GLASS   RED WINE GLASS   WHITE WINE
          (CAN GO TO   (FILL BEFORE   GLASS
          LEFT OF FORKS)   GUESTS SIT
                                                        DOWN)

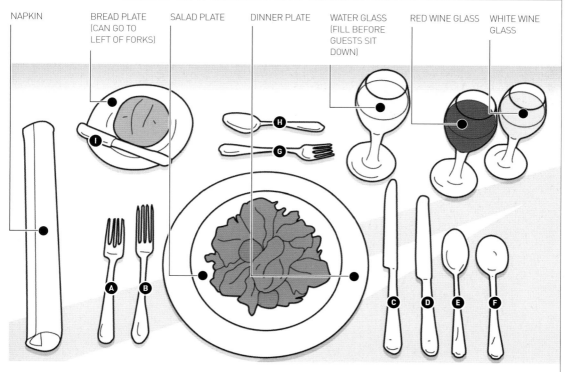

A SALAD FORK	**E** DINNER SPOON	
B MAIN COURSE/DINNER FORK	**F** SOUP SPOON	
C MAIN COURSE/DINNER KNIFE	**G** DESSERT FORK	
D SALAD KNIFE	**H** DESSERT SPOON	
	I BUTTER KNIFE	

Everything in its place

Don't be overwhelmed by all the cutlery and glasses shown in this example. You can aspire to this level of formality and number of courses but settle for a more informal arrangement. When the VP of the company comes for dinner, you'll know what to do. If it's all too much, do a stir-fry and use chopsticks.

Dressing the Table

T he cutlery and glasses are all in place, the seating plan is in your head if not on paper, so all you need now are the finishing touches for the table. Remember to keep it simple, and that details are important.

Use your tablecloth as a canvas. Small flourishes are better than bold moves, so go for a minimalist approach and you will be able to see the person sitting opposite you. It never helps the atmosphere if you have to dodge a jungle of big flowers or negotiate a maze of candelabras and decorative items to embark on a conversation.

Wax lyrical
Add to the atmosphere by placing a couple of small, reasonably short candles at either end of a table that is set for six or eight people. Scented candles work well too. Remember to extinguish all flames (other than romantic ones) when you retire to another room.

A touch of florals
You don't have to be a budding florist to arrange a few flowers successfully, either for the table or sideboard. If panic is rising at the very thought of it, buy a dried flower arrangement. However, fresh stems with a subtle scent can make a table look and smell really good.

Come into the fold
Large cloth napkins are most easily presented by placing them face up, folding them in three length-wise, then folding them in half again. Smaller napkins can be folded into a rectangle twice and then into a triangle. If you are feeling brave and artistic, try the following with a fairly large cloth napkin:

ROLL IT ONCE, ROLL IT TWICE, ROLL IT ALL THE WAY

1

Fold the napkin in half so that the upper and lower edges meet. Then simply roll the napkin from the left side to the centre. Stand back and admire or keep on rollin' from the right.

2

After completing a half roll, turn the napkin over in preparation for the backflip double roll.

3

For the double roll, roll from the right to the centre, so that the two rolls meet half way. Voilà.

4

Place completed backflip double roll to the left of the fork. Double voilà.

FLOWER ARRANGING

Arranging flowers is not as tricky or time-consuming as you may think. It can be quite satisfying and may bring out the artist in you. For a basic arrangement, buy a bunch of colourful flowers at a store or florist and pop them gently into a vase (with water). Before purchase, check that the flowers look as if they will have some life left in them on the day they are due to impress your guests. Don't go for firmly closed buds on the morning of the dinner party. A warm room will help them open but you need to give them a proper chance over a day or two to open out fully.

Braver folk can try their hand at a spot of floral DIY. Think of the following arrangement as a menu for a simple meal using just three ingredients – in this case anemones, tulips and twisted hazel stems. You can be equally successful using different stems and other flowers, depending on what is in season at the time, but try to choose striking, contrasting colours (reds, blues and yellows are always eye-catching). Keep an eye on the overall silhouette of the arrangement (i.e. its width, height, vertical and horizontal lines). This particular arrangement would work well on a table or dresser to the side of the dining table. It should take a beginner a maximum of seven minutes to complete. With experience, it should be done in five.

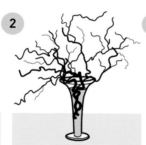

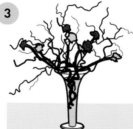

1

- TALL GLASS VASE
- 3 OR 4 STEMS OF TWISTED HAZEL (OR WILLOW)
- ANEMONES (BLUE, ONE BUNCH)
- TULIPS (YELLOW, ONE BUNCH)
- WATER

2

Place twisted stems in the vase firmly. Think of them as the backing group. By the way, if twisted stems are hard to come by or you forget to buy, pop out into the nearest forest and collect some attractive twigs. Very au naturel.

3

Place the anemones one by one among the twigs, followed by the tulips. Don't bunch the blues to one side and the yellows to the other – distribute the colour evenly. This is an integrated arrangement not a contest. The twisted stems will keep the flowers in place, but do ensure that the flowers can get to the water.

4

The tulips may well change shape and position the next day and you will need to adjust accordingly. Place arrangement on side table and mention casually if nobody spots it. Flowers bring colour, scent and perspective to the table and a further dimension to the conversation.

Feeding and Watering Your Guests

C onversation will flow more easily if people can relax, drink in hand, before a meal. Guests are likely to turn up at different times and some may well arrive irritatingly early, but be ready to spoil them anyway. Be prepared with your chosen selection of beverages, be they soft drinks, spirits, aperitifs, cocktails, beer, white wine, red wine or champagne.

DINNER DOS AND DON'TS

BE PREPARED

It's a cliché but it's true in both the kitchen and the dining room: organisation plus preparation equals success (and more time for fun).

STAY COOL

On both personal and culinary levels. Make one course or dish ahead of time and keep it refrigerated until the final garnish and moment of truth. This leaves you more time to attend to your guests and keep up with the conversation

SEASONAL VARIATION

If it's a chilly day, it's fine to serve a heavy soup, followed by a big roast with all the trimmings (see page 88 for carving instructions) and a traditional dessert with lashings of hot custard. However, it's less appetizing when the weather outside is the same temperature as in the oven.

GOOD BEGINNINGS

Serve a light starter, followed by a more substantial main course. Treat the dinner as if it were a rock concert. A good support band will get things going, then build up to the excitement of the headliner with a great main dish. Finally, end on a high note, savouring the dessert encore.

VEGGIE VARIATIONS

Do check if any of your guests don't eat certain things (such as meat, fish, eggs or dairy products) and if they have any particular dislikes or food allergies. It saves awkwardness, embarrassment or panic at the table.

EYE CANDY

Make sure you introduce a variety of colours to the menu – mix reds, yellows, oranges and greens. Think of the plate as a painter's palette. Think tomatoes and basil, green salad and oranges and meat and potatoes for natural taste and style sensations.

SURF AND TURF

This combination can be delicious (such as seafood with steak) but, generally speaking, serve fish and meat dishes separately, fish first, meat second.

OPPOSITES ATTRACT

If one course is very spicy, balance it with a more soothing, milder one. Alternatively, serve buckets of cold water and have the fire extinguishers and indigestion tablets ready.

THE SHAPE OF THINGS TO COME

Try to build up your collection of appropriate glasses, using the following line-up as a guideline:

THE BIG RED

Red wine glasses are generally larger than their white wine counterparts (eyes right). The curvaceous bowl allows you to swirl the wine with abandon, to release its evocative bouquet.

THE FIZZ MACHINE

Long, tall and slender, full of fizz and attractively fragile, the champagne flute is deeply romantic and glamorous. Watch the bubbles rise, clink glasses, say a few romantic words and then try to get your nose in.

THE WHITE KNIGHT

Always hold wine glasses by the stem to avoid adding body warmth to the delicate contents. Enjoy a glass of chilled Chardonnay with your partner on a summer evening or serve a tasty Riesling before dinner.

THE SOCIAL MIXER

If you're on a budget, buy wine glasses that suit both red and white wine and can even be used for serving water. This glass is a social chameleon and adapts to whatever is thrown at it or in it.

MY NAME IS JAMES

Now you're talking. The cocktail glass has an extraordinary glamour and resonance. Martini (shaken or stirred), olive, romance, music, sunset – what more do you need?

THE TUMBLER RUMBLER

Practical, versatile, sturdy, capacious, convenient for the dishwasher (even smart enough for your favourite lager) – the highball is the universal glass. A transparent all-rounder.

JUST A DROP DEAR

If your mother or aunt pops round at 6pm, offer her a glass of chilled sherry served in an elegant, generous glass. Put a few salty snacks in a clean bowl. Make her feel special. Divert her attention from the dust.

UN DIGESTIF, MONSIEUR?

Brandy and cognac demand their own design, known by some as a snifter. They look silly in a wineglass and decadent in a highball. Warm your hands around the bowl if things are rather frosty at the table.

SHORTY BUT NAUGHTY

Drink too much liqueur or schnapps and you'll need a fire extinguisher, hence the diminutive glass. The liquid may be transparent but its intentions are sometimes unclear and its consequences a little fuzzy-edged.

TINY TOT TUMBLER

Small and practical, the mini tumbler can be used for water, juice, cordial or a drop of the stronger stuff, such as whisky or bourbon. It's highly flexible, distinctly friendly and modestly stylish – like its owner, of course.

Good Mixers

T here's no need to be an expert in order to be able to appreciate wine. It's really a matter of deciding what you like and what you don't. Try wines from different countries, sample reds, whites and rosés, light and heavy, mature and young. Trust your own palate and you will gradually find out which grapes, vineyards, and years suit you. Additionally, ask retailers for their advice, check with your friends what they prefer and keep a note of a particularly delicious wine brought by a guest or enjoyed in a restaurant.

COCKTAILS

Any self-respecting barman has a certain amount of equipment and knows how to use it in front of an audience. Keys to success include a stylish cocktail shaker, an ice bucket, interesting glassware, a jigger (measure), lots of crushed ice and an understanding of both timing and performance, Straws and umbrellas up the irony quota. Depending on which cocktail(s) you decide to make, you will need a good supply of the relevant liquor(s), spirits, soda, tonic, fruit juices, cream, olives, limes and sickly-sweet glacé cherries. The good news is that at cocktail parties you generally don't need to feed your guests. Hors d'oeuvres, nuts and pretzels should suffice.

Shake, rattle or roll?
Different cocktails demand different skills. Brush up on who does what to which recipe and you can impress your guests. Be a spirit of the age.

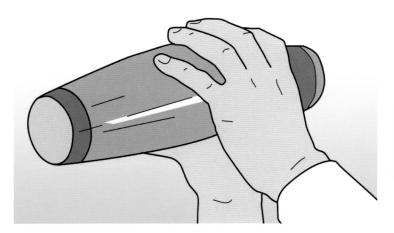

PARTY TRICKS

It's worth having a few tricks up your wine waiter's sleeve when entertaining.

- USE A PROPER CORKSCREW RATHER THAN A DESIGNER MODEL – A LEVER- STYLE 'WAITER'S FRIEND' THAT FITS NEATLY INTO YOUR POCKET IS FINE.

- ALWAYS HAVE ONE ON HAND FOR UNEXPECTED CELEBRATIONS.

- AVOID CORKSCREWS THAT LOOK LIKE MOVING SCULPTURES. THEY ARE MORE 'VAIN' THAN 'VIN'.

- IF THE CORK BREAKS DURING UNCORKING, GO FOR IT – PUSH IT DOWN INTO THE BOTTLE, DECANT THE WINE THROUGH A CLEAN FILTER OR A STRAINER.

- DECANT HEAVIER RED WINES (BORDEAUX, SHIRAZ, BURGUNDY, PINOT NOIR AND CHIANTI) AND PORT INTO A DECANTER TO LET THEM BREATHE AND EXPAND IN FLAVOUR FOR A COUPLE OF HOURS. IF THERE IS SEDIMENT AT THE BOTTOM OF THE BOTTLE, STOP POURING JUST BEFORE YOU GET TO IT.

- WHITE WINES DO NOT NEED DECANTING. DON'T SERVE THEM TOO COLD, AS THIS WILL BLUNT THEIR FLAVOUR, AND AVOID CHILLING THEM IN THE FREEZER AS CHANCES YOU ARE, YOU'LL FORGET YOU PUT THEM THERE.

- WHEN OPENING CHAMPAGNE OR SPARKLING WINE IN FRONT OF ASSEMBLED GUESTS OR A SPECIAL PERSON, TAKE CARE NOT TO WASTE THE BUBBLES. AVOID SHAKING THE BOTTLE AND MAKE SURE IT IS WELL CHILLED. PEEL OFF THE FOIL CAPSULE, LOOSEN THE METAL WIRE AND KEEP ONE HAND OVER THE CORK, IN CASE IT POPS OFF. HOLD THE BOTTLE AT A 45-DEGREE ANGLE, LOOSEN THE CORK ENOUGH TO LET SOME GAS ESCAPE BY GENTLY TWISTING THE BASE OF THE BOTTLE WITH ONE HAND AND PUSHING UP THE CORK WITH YOUR THUMB.

- MATCH FOOD WITH DRINK. A LUSTY, HEARTY RED WINE, SUCH AS A CABERNET SAUVIGNON, WILL GET ON WELL WITH RED MEAT AND STEWS BETTER THAN A LIGHT WINE. LIGHTER FOOD FINDS BALANCE WITH LIGHTER WHITE OR RED WINES. A RIESLING GOES WELL WITH TUNA, A LIGHT PINOT NOIR MEETS ITS MATCH WITH SALMON, BUT A HEAVIER ONE LIKES TO BE SEEN WITH DUCK OR GAME. FISH, CHICKEN AND PASTA ENJOY THE COMPANY OF A CHARDONNAY. A HEAVIER RED WINE MAY SHOW OFF ITS BIG PERSONALITY WHEN IT MEETS LIGHTER FOOD BUT THAT DOESN'T HAVE TO BE A BAD THING. SPICY OR SWEET FOOD GENERALLY LIKES TO GO HAND IN HAND WITH A SWEETER WINE.

DOMESTIC GOD
THE PERFECT BUCK'S FIZZ

In 1921, a certain Mr McGarry of Buck's Club in London felt suddenly inspired to mix one part orange juice with two parts chilled champagne and add a dash of grenadine. The Buck's Fizz was born. Although a simple affair, it is glamorous and evocative, perfect for getting a dinner party or a sunny Sunday morning with your beloved off to a good start. Serve in a fluted glass and wait for the bubbles to rise (you can fake it with sparkling wine or Cava instead). If you don't finish the whole bottle, don't worry – it will retain its bubbles overnight in the refrigerator without a stopper (or a silver spoon).

Carving a Whole Chicken

O nce you have mastered carving, you will want to do it in front of your guests. A couple of test runs are a good idea. Rehearse with housemates before doing a live performance. Sometimes it's cool to be chicken in order to avoid looking a turkey.

Remove the chicken from the oven, place on a carving board and cover loosely with foil. Allow to 'rest' for about 15 minutes. This allows the juices to sink into the flesh, resulting in plump, moist meat. Place the bird on a carving board with a well to catch the juices and remove any trussing strings. Spoon any stuffing into a serving dish and keep warm. Use any juices for pan-gravy.

ROLL IT ONCE, ROLL IT TWICE, ROLL IT ALL THE WAY

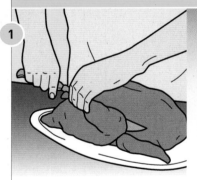

1 Using a carving knife (or an electric one if you haven't been to the gym for a few days), cut through the skin between the thigh and body.

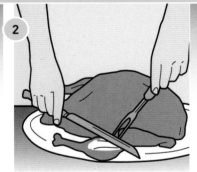

2 Continue cutting until you reach the ball-and-socket joint, then twist the leg away from the body. Cut the drumstick and thigh apart.

4 Hold thigh firmly on plate with a fork and cut slices of meat parallel to the bone.

5 Cut off the wing. Carve the other side. Arrange the wings and slices on the serving plate. Smile. Make a deep cut into the breast close to the wing.

LEFTOVER LAWS

Put leftover turkey or chicken in the refrigerator as soon as possible, removing the flesh from the bones first. Don't leave the carcass in the dining room overnight – the meat needs to get back into the refrigerator within a couple of hours. Eat the leftovers within three days maximum. You can freeze sliced turkey or chicken (put it in a proper storage container), but do use it within one month or evict it from the house. Remember the UFO theory (see page 24).

KNOW YOUR KNIVES

Knives come in all sorts of sizes. Like soccer players they have individual skills. Here's the pre-match line-up.

Chef's knife:
Efficient at chopping and cutting, invaluable asset.

Carving or slicing knife:
Indispensable for slicing thinly. Cutting-edge player.

Serrated bread knife
A cut above the rest with bread, puts tomatoes in the back of the net.

Sharpening steel
Keeps everyone on their toes, a player manager with a sharp tongue.

Paring knife
Good at peeling and detailed manoeuvres. A team player.

Utility knife
Great all-rounder, likes vegetables. A valuable player.

Boning knife
Tough and versatile. Good to have on the bench.

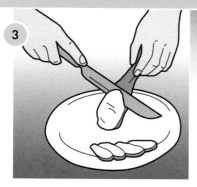

3 Hold the drumstick upright, at a convenient angle to the plate and cut down, turning the drumstick in order to get uniform slices.

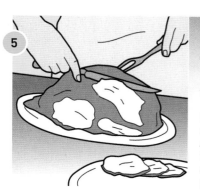

5 Beginning at the front, halfway up the breast, cut thin slices of white meat.

Mission accomplished. Await applause from impressed and hungry guests.

HOME OFFICE

Entertaining Stuff
Make room for a place to sit and think or to greet guests.

Plant Life
Improve the working atmosphere with houseplants but remember to take care of them.

Paper Chase
Establish an efficient filing system. Keep paperwork on desk to a minimum. Ensure floor remains free of piles of paper.

'A PIECE OF PAPER CAN BE GOOD OR BAD NEWS.
A PILE OF PAPER IS ALWAYS OLD NEWS.'

Mark Roberts

Sitting Pretty
Ensure your chair is at the right height.

Screen Clean
Dust your computer every week.

Home Office

N owadays, more and more people are working from home and enjoying some distinct advantages over their office-bound chums. Gone is the corporate jungle, the dress code, the compulsory air-conditioning and the awful coffee. There are disadvantages too, of course. You spend much more time alone, you can't delegate, there's nobody to do your filing and the cleaners don't clear up your mess.

It's likely that your home office forms part of another space or is squeezed into the smallest room in the home rather than having been specially interior designed for the purpose. Whatever the case, use the area you have economically and ergonomically. Don't put your computer in front of a large window – ideally, the window should be to your right or left. A window directly behind you could cause glare. A good desk lamp is important, keep the lighting soft, flicker-free and indirect and ensure you have a proper chair and a comfortable keyboard at the correct height.

And keep things under control by watching out for a few no-nos.

CHORE CHART: WHAT TO DO WHEN

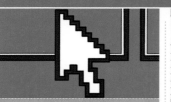

DAILY:
- CLEAR AND CLEAN DESK
- SORT INCOMING MAIL – ACT, FILE OR TRASH
- JUNK THE JUNK MAIL
- REMOVE OLD COFFEE CUPS AND PLATES
- MANAGE EMAILS (CYBER HOUSEWORK)
- BACK UP FILES (CYBER LARDER)
- TRASH THE TRASH

WEEKLY:
- SWEEP OR VACUUM FLOORS
- DUST COMPUTER SCREEN
- WIPE SURFACES
- CARE FOR HOUSEPLANTS
- SORT PAPER FOR RECYCLING
- DO FILING

MONTHLY:
- CLEAN COMPUTER KEYBOARD AND SCREEN
- DUST SHELVES AND WINDOWSILLS
- CLEAN WINDOWS
- CHECK INK AND STATIONERY SUPPLIES
- MANAGE AND EDIT FILES
- DEAL WITH RECYCLING
- VACUUM AND SWEEP THOROUGHLY
- WASH PAINTWORK

X NO-NOS

A tidy office is an efficient office. Keep clutter to a minimum and the working day will seem considerably shorter.

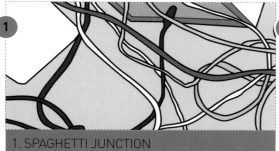

1. SPAGHETTI JUNCTION

You may have escaped the corporate jungle, but don't replace it with a forest of wires and cables. Your networking is clearly not functioning if you trip over a maze of spaghetti-like leads on a daily basis. Trailing wires are hazardous, unsightly and won't impress anyone who visits, either on a professional or personal basis. Label each wire with an appropriate sticker, tie them all together safely and then conceal them from view as much as possible with tubes or covers. And keep pets away.

2. NO STAIN, BIG GAIN

If you must slurp coffee while at your desk, take care not to spill it over your paperwork, desktop or, most importantly, your keyboard. If you are particularly clumsy, invest in a plastic protective cover (available from most office supplies stores). Don't leave nasty-looking cups of congealed coffee and tea on the desk (or anywhere else for that matter, see page 59) – all you will achieve is an unpleasant stain. Be nice to the office cleaner – remember, it's you.

3. THE KEY ISSUE

Keyboards and computer screens provide refuge for dust, dirt, crumbs, and fingerprints, while all kinds of microbes can set up home in their crevices. Regular dusting is the answer. Use a large, soft brush or clean cotton buds to displace dust between the keys on your keyboard or a spray can of compressed air. Remove fingerprints on your screen with a slightly damp cloth, but always remember to turn the computer off first. Keep computers out of direct sunlight as it may cause them to overheat.

4. PAPER MOUNTAINS

Business-like equals business ace (as some multi-millionaire once said). Creativity is great in the Creative Department but not in Accounts. Space taken up by paper of no fixed abode, trays and boxes of no fixed purpose and piles of no fixed order are not fixed assets. Junk must be accounted for – remember, you are paying its rent. Eviction day has come.

Mountains to Molehills: Paperwork Gets the Chop

A desk strewn with paperwork is not necessarily an indication of someone piling through an impressive workload, so keep it under control with organization and a little determination. First the in-tray: use a concertina file labelled with numbers 1-31 to prioritize and diarize its contents. Place on your desk only the things that are in urgent need of action today, tomorrow or by the end of the week. Move tasks forward into pole position once you have completed others – it is a satisfying strategy. Secondly, clear the out-tray – distribute its contents into the post, the filing tray or the trash. Do a little each day and it won't build up into a big pile.

CLUTTER-BUSTING

EXAMINE YOUR DRAWERS

Is there a nasty mess within? If so, clear it out by being ruthless and unsentimental. Next, insert a tray with different compartments inside or just divide the drawer in half, placing things you use regularly at the front. Hanging files work well in deep drawers for documents you use regularly. Spring clean them regularly.

FILE STYLE

Look at your filing system – is it categorised? Is one file so thick you can't shut it or open it properly? Are some of the documents older than the cat? Sub-divide files into 'Past' and 'Present.' Keep vital papers to hand and store the rest. Review your files regularly. Label them clearly. Arrange in an alphabetical order on the shelf.

Here's my card

Don't collect business cards like stamps – they don't increase in value, but do decrease in accuracy and use up space. Glue or staple those you want to keep to alphabetized cards on a rotating filing system and add any useful information. You then have a mini-profile of customers or suppliers on hand whenever you need it. Put household details in there, too, such as the telephone numbers of the plumber, electrician, doctor and vet.

Electronic storage

Use your computer for effective storage. Invest in the best back-up software you can afford and use it properly. Think of your computer as a cyber house and files as rooms within it. You need to create order, apply safety precautions and protect your investment, so do a spring clean from time to time.

OLD NEWS

If you subscribe to a number of professional magazines or periodicals, throw out or recycle those older than six months. Cut out any important articles and file them appropriately.

EMERGENCY EXIT

In the event that you might have to leave your home very quickly, keep important documents (such as passports, birth certificates, credit card details, investment records, insurance and tax papers) in one sub-divided file in a fireproof safe. You could store copies of them in the bank to be doubly sure.

OPENING THE POST

Open your post close to where your concertina file and recycling box or bin are within easy reach. Junk mail and non-reusable envelopes can go straight inside one or the other (save the stamps for philatelists or charities). Bills needing attention within the next 7-14 days can slot straight into the relevant part of the concertina file and be systematically promoted in the league of importance. Bills needing immediate attention must go into the in-tray, where only tasks requiring urgent action belong. Do today what's in the in-tray, is a useful mantra to follow.

IN, OUT AND FILE – THE PAPER TRAIL

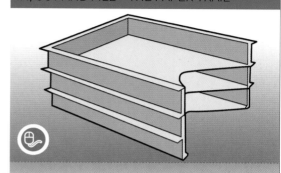

Use a three-tier filing system to keep paper under control. Put urgent documents and bills in the one marked 'In' (and place in concertina file according to urgency). This is located on the top level for a practical reason – documents remain within view and in with a chance of being dealt with. Put things that need to be distributed or sent out in the 'Out' tray. Out of sight does not mean out of mind or out of control, however. The low-level tray is for filing. Don't let it build up and up until it nudges the 'Out' tray from below, like an elephant in a child-sized bunk bed.

Make space pay

If your office were a shop floor, every little inch of it would have to justify itself in terms of profit. Dead space, horizontal and vertical, is unprofitable. Look around you – if you see a chaotic jigsaw of multi-coloured notes on the noticeboard with names and numbers of people you can't remember and forgotten motivational mantras, then deal with them. Focus – free up space to free up your mind. When you have cleared the surfaces, give them a clean.

Divide and rule

If you sort your paperwork out as soon as it arrives it won't end up in a frightening heap, paralyzing you. If you don't deal with it on arrival, you will waste time looking for it later. Just think how many hours you have wasted by looking for an invoice and how much stress you have endured worrying about where you put that big cheque. Where's that business card with the Vice President's home number on it? Compare these feelings of frustration, impatience and anxiety with the satisfaction to be derived from sorting out bills, sending cheques and paying them in on the day they arrive or need to be dealt with. Paperwork D.O.A. doesn't have to mean dead on arrival. Deal on Arrival gives you your life back.

Focus

Focussed
Operations
Can
Unblock
Space

Look at the floor and surfaces in your office. Guess how many pieces of paper are lying around? Sorry, no prizes for the right quantity. What you have to do now is imagine that they have been picked up, sorted, filed, trashed or recycled. What a great feeling. Back to reality. Clear the clutter. Pick up the paper. Deal with the documents. Trash the trash. Recycle the remains. Once you can see the carpet, vacuum it. Put a comfortable chair in the new paper-free zone you have created. Use it for reading long documents, doing hard-copy research or just thinking away from your computer (you don't have to be a screen lover from dawn to dusk). Ask guests to sit comfortably instead of perching on an old cardboard box you haven't emptied since you set up your office. You see, things are looking better already.

HOW IT WORKS:

Houseplants and Their Owners

T hink of your home as a mini earth, equipped with a range of different climatic conditions. Your bathroom is a humid rainforest, your kitchen a steamy jungle and your living room a warm, sunny, dry zone. You need to see plants not as isolated, pretty objects that bring a spot of colour or scent to your home, but as part of the living domestic ecosystem. Your job as an indoor gardener is to create mini ecosystems that provide sufficient light, water, food and warmth and choose the plants that suit those conditions. Think of your houseplant as a housemate. Putting a cactus in the bathroom would be like asking your housemate to live in the cupboard under the stairs. The idea might appeal at first but it is not going to be a long-standing relationship. Something will wilt and fade.

CHOOSE WITH CARE:

Don't buy the first pretty plant you come across. Consider the room it is destined for – check the temperature, humidity, intensity and direction of light – and then look at the plant suitability tag or ask the retailer's advice. Choose a plant with clean, healthy-looking foliage and no signs of pest, disease or discoloration. A light, airy office is good for plants. Position a plant within the room with care – near a window against a white wall equals a straight plant, whereas a dark wall reflects no light, making the plant lean towards the window as a source of light.

FOOD OF LOVE:

You need to feed indoor plants with fertilizer, in liquid, pellet or powdered form. Amounts will depend on size and variety, but the larger and more vigorous the plant, the more food it will need. Check the underside of your plant's leaves frequently for pests, such as spider mites.

RULE OF THUMB:

To detect when to water, press your thumb into the soil to test moisture content and only water when it feels dry. If the soil loses touch with the sides of the container, you left it rather late. To revive a dehydrated plant, loosen the top layer of soil to allow the water to permeate to the roots. Water the plant thoroughly and spray the leaves with tepid water.

Cleaning leaves:

Yes, houseplants involve housework, but not too much. Hardy plants with glossy leaves, such as the rubber plant, can be cleaned by sponging the leaves with a damp cloth. Don't use detergent and wipe only the well developed leaves, not the soft, new ones. Use one hand to support the leaf when wiping it firmly but not harshly. Smaller plants with hairy leaves (such as the African Violet) need gentle treatment and should not be cleaned with liquid or chemicals. Use a soft brush to lightly dust the surface.

HANDLE WITH CARE:

Watering is key to caring for your houseplant. Too much water and the root system will be unable to breathe, causing yellowed leaves, rot and death. Too little water and the plant will also die. Use tepid water for plant watering. Pour enough water onto the top of the soil for surplus to accumulate in the pot in which the plant is standing. Do not let the plant stand in this water for any length of time. The warmer the room, the greater the evaporation, and the stronger the plant performs, the more water it will require.

WHICH PLANT WHERE?

Living room
Plants such as cacti like it hot and dry, so put them in the living room. Water sparingly in the winter months when they rest but bump up the supply in the spring. Succulents don't like to be waterlogged and will rot if you allow them to stand in water.

Bathroom and kitchen
It can get steamy or damp in these rooms and the African violet just adores humidity. It reminds it of the faraway, misty coastal forests of home. Don't overwater the violet though, because, like your bathroom, it needs good drainage. If your bathroom is shady, try a maidenhair fern, for which home is the tropical forest. Try growing a selection of your favourite herbs on a kitchen windowsill or balcony. Sweet basil, parsley and chives do well in pots. Hyacinths and amaryllises love the sun and orchids are generally happy on a windowsill with a sunny outlook, but need misting during the growing season. A touch of natural fragrance in the bathroom is a good idea.

Dark and shady spots
Palms like dark shady corners and put up a good fight against draughts, too much or too little water and fumes from open fires. They are pretty low-maintenance and undemanding.

Home office
Plants make you feel better at work – literally. Some people have up to ten house plants in their home offices. They absorb pollutants and gases, especially carbon monoxide, a main constituent of cigarette smoke. They make perfect air-conditioners, eco-style. If your home office were big enough to take a tree, it would do wonders for your work environment. Plants are an easier option. Fragrant plants encourage you to breathe more deeply, thereby relaxing you more when nasty emails come in.

If a plant fails to thrive in your chosen location, don't give up. Just move it to a different spot and see how it does. Homes with central heating are not perfect environments for plants that need humidity, but you can help by placing the pot on wet stones or near saucers of water. Mist its leaves from time to time, too.

Pets in the Office and at Home

T hose of you who have a pet will know that it offers unconditional love, non-judgmental companionship and unquestioning loyalty in return for a bowl of food twice a day, a quick romp in the park, regular brushing and a comfy place to sleep. Cats and dogs (and maybe even fish) are always delighted to see you. They are also good for your health according to Australian research that shows how pet owners are less at risk of heart disease and high blood pressure than non-owners. In addition, pets are known to boost spirits and relieve depression.

It is important that your pet fits in with your lifestyle, temperament and living space. A large, excitable dog and an absentee owner in a small urban apartment is not a perfect love match. Remember too that the arrival of a pet brings extra household chores. You need to establish a few house rules if this relationship is going to work.

HELPFUL HYGIENE

- TRY TO LIMIT YOUR PET TO CERTAIN ROOMS IN THE HOUSE AND ESTABLISH ONE PET-FREE ZONE. KEEP YOUR PET CLEAN BY REGULARLY BRUSHING AND WASHING.
- WASH YOUR HANDS AFTER STROKING YOUR PET AND DON'T TOUCH YOUR EYES BEFORE YOUR HANDS ARE ABSOLUTELY CLEAN.
- EACH TO THEIR OWN: DON'T SHARE BOWLS OR PLATES WITH YOUR PET. BUY YOUR PET AN ATTRACTIVE BOWL AND MAKE SURE EVERYONE IN THE HOUSE USES IT FOR ROVER OR FELIX.
- WASH YOUR BEDDING THOROUGHLY IF YOUR CAT OR DOG MANAGES TO CLIMB ONTO YOUR BED.
- IF YOU SUFFER FROM ALLERGIC CONJUNCTIVITIS, TRY WEARING SUNGLASSES DURING SPECIAL MOMENTS WITH YOUR PET. THEY WON'T LAUGH AT YOU.

DO-DOS AND NO-NOS

DO-DOS ✔

Invest in your pet:
A wise investment generally leads to dividends. Consider it a 'petfolio.' Spend time with your pet each day, buy it toys and chews, install a padded perch near a sunny window for your cat or a comfortable place for your dog to relax. Plant cat grass in indoor pots for your feline friend so it can graze. Buy a ready-made cat tree for climbing opportunities. A happy pet is more likely to be a safe one.

Breed needs
Do some serious research about the breed of dog that suits your circumstances. How much space, time and energy can you devote to it? Think about the pet rather than yourself when you do this. Dogs are portrayed in the media as ornaments, trophies and fashion statements. If this is what you want, get a battery-operated pet. A proper relationship with a pet has to be a two-way street, a mutual affair involving care, compromise and commitment.

Toxic plants
Do choose your houseplants with care – some can be toxic. Cats like to dig in the soil and can be harmed by certain plants. Do some research or consult your vet.

Close the doors and keep a lid on it
If you want to keep pets out of certain areas, keep the doors to those rooms firmly closed. Some animals enjoy messing about with trash. Keep it safe from their paws, claws and jaws.

On all fours
Scan your home for possible hazards – shoes, smelly socks, sharp pencils, paper clips, important documents, expensive briefcases, chewable computer wires and cords, designer footwear. Pick up and store or protect all of the aforementioned items.

Fish deserve respect
A goldfish bowl is only a temporary home for Goldie – his or her (how do you tell?) permanent address should be a correct-sized aquarium complete with plants, a pump and toys etc. Clean it once a month, don't overfeed Goldie and if you use tap water, check if chemicals need to be added to remove the chlorine.

Fire, flames and fur
Never leave your pet alone in a room with a lit candle or an unattended fire. Animals are attracted to the bright lights and can knock the candles over, spilling hot wax onto the carpet and themselves, and creating a fire hazard.

Boney bits
Be wary of giving your pets the leftovers of a roast dinner. Chicken bones can be lethal for cats and dogs.

Christmas hazards
Don't hang Christmas decorations on the lower branches of your tree. If pets eat tinsel, they can choke. Replace metal ornament hooks with fabric ribbons or twine, and don't let them eat holly, ivy or mistletoe.

Beware medication and chocolate
Keep all medication out of your pet's reach. Even small doses of human drugs can be lethal for animals. And don't feed them chocolate – it can be poisonous.

Mind muddy paws
Don't let muddy paws create a new pattern on your carpet. Wipe paws before they have a chance to make a mess, or invent some shoes for dogs.

Phone calls
Cats like to chew most things, but cordless phones with aerials are up there at the top of their list of favourites, along with remote controls for dogs. Keep all these items safe.

Litter alert
Litter boxes require regular attention. Change the litter every day or every other day (depending on the temperature outside) or as soon as you detect an unpleasant odour. Keep the box away from food preparation areas and in a well-ventilated space, such as a utility room or garage. The box needs to be washed frequently – outside if possible. Pet cages need regular attention too, with bedding that needs changing just like ours.

Don't forget
A pet is forever. You can't send your pet an email saying it's all over. Establish and enjoy this potentially highly rewarding relationships. However, don't let your pet kiss you on the lips. Keep those kisses for your partner.

Dust, wipe and vacuum
This tried and trusted trio plays an even more important role in households with pets. If you don't have time to indulge in these three activities twice a week, perform them as often as you can to control hair and allergens. Vacuuming will rid your home of pet fleas, which are fairly common. Place particular focus on the area in and around where your pet sleeps.

BEDROOM

Declutter
Keep bedroom clutter to a minimum to ensure a good night's sleep. Hang up and store your clothes at the end of the day. Vacuum the floor every week .

Bed Behaviour
Wash your bedlinen regularly, particularly your pillow case. Make sure your pets know your bed is a no-go area.

'A CAPTAIN IN THE KITCHEN IS OFTEN
A BRIGADIER IN THE BEDROOM.'

A. Ellis

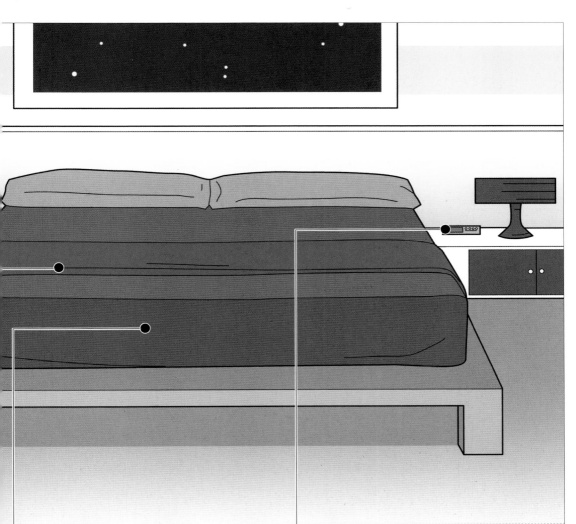

Mattress Management
Turn and vacuum your mattress to
keep dust mites at bay.

Appliances
Limit electrical appliances to
the essentials.

In the Bedroom

The bedroom is a very private, personal space. When things get on top of you in other rooms or in the big bad world outside, seeking sanctuary in the bedroom is often a natural and successful strategy. It's important to feel safe and secure within it, safe enough to give free rein to your emotions, imagination and sexual feelings, and secure enough to be naked, both physically and spiritually, to peel off your daytime mask, shed suit, tie or uniform and just be.

Before you sleep, perchance to dream (as the great Bard said), check out a few of these important No-Nos.

CHORE CHART: WHAT TO DO WHEN

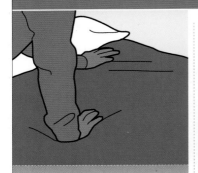

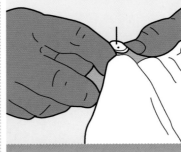

DAILY:
- AIR BOTH BED AND ROOM
- MAKE BED
- SORT AND REMOVE DIRTY LAUNDRY
- HANG UP CLOTHES
- TIDY ROOM
- REMOVE CUPS, GLASSES AND PLATES

WEEKLY:
- CHANGE BEDLINEN (OR EVERY FORTNIGHT)
- WASH PILLOWCASES
- VACUUM OR SWEEP FLOOR
- DUST SHELVES
- CLEAN SURFACES
- SORT OUT DRYCLEANING

MONTHLY:
- TURN AND VACUUM MATTRESS
- CLEAN WINDOWS
- VACUUM THOROUGHLY
- WASH PAINTWORK
- TIDY CLOSET
- REPAIR CLOTHES

X NO-NOS

1. BED BUGS

Don't try to run your office from bed by creating a mini HQ between the sheets. Laptops in bed are a no-no, as are mobile phones, too many remote controls, briefcases and work files. Pillow talk isn't dangerous, so press the Think key and keep it simple. If you and your partner are in bed but glued to separate phones, you are obviously moving along different lines and action is required.

2. DAMP SQUIBS

Leaving a wet towel on the bed does no one any favours. It's a careless action that's both unthinking and unhygienic, leaving an unnecessary damp patch on the sheets or bedcover and preventing either the towel or bedding from drying and airing properly. It doesn't help the atmosphere in the room – on any level. The moisture becomes trapped, unable to evaporate, thereby creating a perfect environment for unpleasant microbes and mould-makers to move in and multiply. It takes seconds to hang up a wet towel, so what's the big deal?

3. WHISK US AWAY

You can be forgiven for leading pets to believe they are the most precious things in your life, but they should be banned from the bedroom, especially if you suffer from allergies. Teddies and soft toys collect dust too, and create clutter, so don't turn your bedroom into a small zoo. Animal instincts of a different kind are fine but no impostors please.

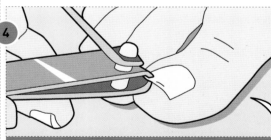

4. NAIL IT ON THE HEAD

Clipping your toenails in bed is unthinkable, right? It is about the worst personal habit you could indulge in and impose on others. Toenails are at the most southerly point of the body for a very good reason – that of distance. The amputated, offending articles should not be seen anywhere near the bedroom. If toenails are between the sheets, romance won't be. End of discussion.

Bediquette

t has been calculated that humans spend around one third of their lives in bed, but this doesn't mean that one third of our belongings have to join us. The bedrooms should be a womb-like space that provides refuge and sanctuary and the simple essentials needed for our development, just like the real thing.

Simplicity is key, so banish random memorabilia, photographs, trophies or childhood clutter and stick to uncomplicated decoration and clean lines. In general, you will feel safer and healthier in a simply equipped and furnished bedroom. Don't worry if your bedroom is rather small. It can create a sense of security and intimacy that larger rooms don't supply so easily. As a result, vacuuming takes less time and who's complaining?

GOOD BED, BAD BED

A bad bed is unmade, unclean, untidy, unhygienic, uninviting and in some cases unrecognisable. You won't sleep well in a bed with dirty, crumpled sheets. If it's full of books, videos, magazines and crumbs (and they are just the identifiable objects), you are quite likely to sleep alone, except for the uninvited guests with several legs and even more unpleasant habits. Brush the sheets regularly (or simply change them), air the bed and the room every day and put the mess where it belongs – in the trash or in another room. Compare the images below – which room looks the most appealing?

A good bed is clean, tidy, smooth, fragrant, hygienic, inviting and minimalist. Its sole purpose is to offer a sound and healthy night's sleep. Warm it up with a blast of hot air from your hairdryer on a cold night. Make sure your pillows are supportive – they should resume their original shape after you have punched them gently on both sides. Make sure you are not sleeping under too many bedclothes. Change the weight of your quilt with the season. Just use a sheet when it is very warm. Reduce the contents of the room and the bed space to a minimum for maximum comfort.

BEFORE

AFTER

Clean and tidy

Next time you are in bed and about to switch the lights out, scan the room and consider its contents and layout. Perform a mental check of how you feel – restful, anxious, claustrophobic, a bit overwhelmed by all the stuff you alone or you and your partner have accumulated? Is there just too much of it? Try removing some of the clutter, a little every day, first thing in the morning and last thing at night. It's surprising how your mood will improve. Limit electrical goods to the minimum, keeping only things that are strictly necessary or have a positive effect on you.

Banish redundant or little-used equipment such as a television set, music system, computer, radio, foot spa and exercise bike. Discard the things that attract more dust than attention and keep only what makes you feel good. Everything should justify its share of the space. Remember, less clutter, less dust, less effort, more time to relax. Great result.

Keep it light and airy

Damp, poorly ventilated spaces make perfect environments for nasty little mites, allergens and bedbugs to flourish, so introduce clean air into the bedroom at regular intervals. Open wide the windows as often as you can. Allow the room to gulp in fresh and positive supplies of oxygen and expel dust. Airing your bedding is a good idea, too, and sunlight helps to do this while zapping dust mites and lifting your mood, thereby killing two birds and a million critters with one helpful stone.

Keep the room temperature relatively cool and don't smoke in bed – fumes and nasty smells both linger and offend. Don't hang up your wet clothes to dry in your room. Remember your bedroom is a sanctuary for you and your relationship and should be respected as such. Don't pollute it unnecessarily either with noise such as snoring (if you can help it), loud music, phone calls and smelly clothes. The KISS (Keep It Simple, Stupid) rule, if ignored, can result in exactly the opposite.

The oxygen of love

Relationships need space and room to breathe just like real rooms. Claustrophobic, cluttered or unhealthy, oxygen-starved atmospheres won't help them flourish. During your sleeping hours, your body takes in oxygen and emits carbon dioxide (exactly the reverse of plants, in fact); you sweat, exude oils, shed skin. It's all perfectly natural so don't be embarrassed, but do take action to avoid the atmosphere becoming stale, dusty and singularly uninviting.

And this is my room...

Introducing someone to your inner space for the first time, whether with platonic or romantic intent, is an act of intimacy, not unlike allowing someone to take a peek inside your underwear drawer. Imagine what they may find, what their first impression would be and whether they would ever fancy another look.

DON'T BUG ME!

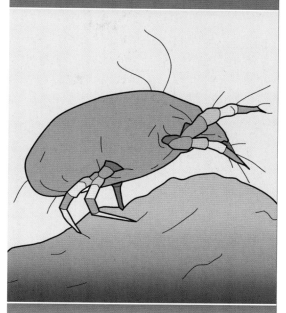

Did you sleep well last night? You might want to clean up your nocturnal act a bit before getting back into bed tonight. You may have shared your very personal space with up to 2 million dust mites. Bed bugs lurk there too, keen to suck your blood and cause itches and rashes. Bacteria with long, difficult names such as staphylococcus and enterococcus are ready to do their unsavoury thing at any time, causing throat infections and diarrhoea respectively if not respectfully. You wouldn't want to introduce them to your partner with names like that would you? Vacuum your mattress regularly if you want to sleep alone.

Shake, rattle or roll?

Every year, humans shed about 500 g (1 lb) of skin scales. Next time you buy a packet of flour equivalent to this weight, imagine it full of skin. Double it if you have a partner. Add a bit more if you have children. Mentally chuck in a few cans of perspiration and bodily oils and you will quickly see the need for bedroom hygiene.

The Bedroom Routine

Bed and breakfast

Bedding should be aired daily, so you don't have to make your bed as soon as you get up. Instead, pull back the bedcovers (no, don't throw them on the floor) and let everything breathe while you prepare for the day. After breakfast, return to the bedroom, smooth your sheets and blankets, plump the pillows (see page 104 for plumping technique) and pull up the cover. Any abandoned clothing on the bed, floor or chair should be put under the pillow, filed in the laundry basket or hung up in the wardrobe. Open the curtains or lift the blinds and, if possible, open a window. Let the sun and air do their thing while you do yours.

Undress your bed

In an ideal world, you would change your sheets and pillowcases every week. If this is not feasible, every two weeks is just about OK, but do try to launder your pillowcase weekly. Remember

that it is in the direct firing line of perspiration, tears, oil and saliva for a third of your day. You may choose to sleep with a top sheet under the duvet, in which case it's quite easy to pop it in the wash with your pillowcase, or, alternatively, swap the top and bottom-sheets around and wash the latter every week.

If you use a blanket regularly, make sure it is dry-cleaned once a year. Take down- or feather-filled duvets and pillows to a specialist cleaner annually too. Bedding with synthetic fillings is washable. If you accidentally spill something on a pillow or duvet that has a natural filling, shake the filling away from the target area and sponge it clean. A mattress cover should protect it from most accidents or spills, but should it become soiled make sure you don't get it too wet when sponging clean or you will get the inside of the mattress wet – a perfect invitation for mould and damp to move in. Wash pillow protectors, mattress covers and duvet covers (if you sleep under a top-sheet) once every month or two.

HORIZONTAL HARMONY

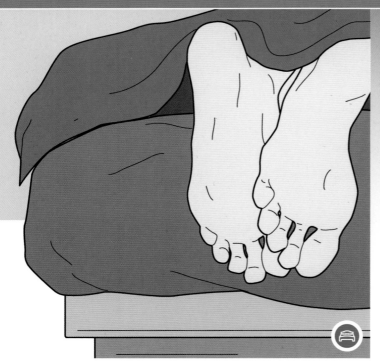

Look after your bed properly and it will look after you. Mattresses have a natural life of around 10 years, so if you want a full decade of use, here's what to do: Turn the mattress from time to time to prevent hollows forming in your usual sleeping position and every three months, turn it top-to-bottom. Vacuum the mattress and pillows regularly. Airing your mattress outside will help keep it fresh and mite-free. If this is not practical, ensure you use mattress and pillow protectors, remembering to launder them regularly. Duvets and pillows should be aired outdoors occasionally too. Take off all the covers, give the duvet and pillows a good shake and leave them in the sun for a couple of hours. If you don't have a garden, hang bedding out of your window.

MAKE YOUR BED AND LIE IN IT

A few top tips for making your bed:

Smooth operator

There is nothing worse than a bottom sheet that looks and feels more like a 3D contour map of the Himalayas, so once in place, ensure your bottom and top-sheets are smooth and wrinkle-free. Fitted bottom sheets can be a challenge, too, but fix one corner at a time and you will get there.

Fold it over

If you like to use a top sheet covered by a blanket, fold the sheet over the blanket at the top so that you don't drool all over it during the night.

Tuck it in

A top-sheet used with a duvet or blanket should be tucked neatly and snugly at each corner, over an unfitted bottom sheet. This will avoid 'frozen foot syndrome' at 3am. Mitred or hospital corners are quite technical – date a nurse to find out more.

Duvet dilemma

Fighting with your duvet or quilt cover as you struggle to fit it is a common source of annoyance and frustration. It is actually quite a simple exercise. Turn the cover inside out and slide your arms inside so that the material is bunched along the length of your arm. Find the corners of the cover, grab the relevant corners of the duvet and slide the cover on, shaking it down as you go. Alternatively, attach pegs to the first two corners as you place the duvet inside and shake down. Now you have got that covered, place a bedcover over the whole bed and stand back to admire your efficient work.

PS: Don't forget to dust and vacuum your room thoroughly once a week too.

DOMESTIC GOD

Always fasten your duvet cover before washing in order to avoid socks and underwear running for cover inside it in the rough and tumble of the washing machine.

Closet Encounters

C lose your eyes, take a mental stroll through your house, opening each door. Which one do you want to close immediately, engulfed by horror and shame? The answer is probably the one that hides the room in which your clothes are struggling to survive, a multi-coloured, mismatched shoal of sardines competing for space and air. Just like humans, clothes enjoy both vertical and horizontal positions. Just like humans, they deserve respect. Treat them mean, keep them keen simply doesn't do it for clothes. Treat them right, they'll last night after night – now you're talking.

Vertical or horizontal?

Woollen clothes like to be horizontal. Fold knitted garments carefully and keep them on a narrow rather than a deep shelf, or in a drawer with room to breathe. Ensure they are clean before putting them away or the stains will attract moths, keen to convert your clothes into sieves. Hanging up wool pulls it out of shape and can cause hemlines to sag. Ironed shirts on the other hand should be kept vertical – they do not appreciate being stuffed, creased and crumpled in to any old place. Hang shirts on hangers with space between them and they will crease less. Smart move all round.

Before you go to bed, fold and hang your trousers, after emptying all pockets and removing the belt. This avoids sagging and bulging in inappropriate areas and is useful for jacket pockets, too. You could try hanging a complete outfit on one hanger in readiness for the next day, particularly if your partner has a later start than yours and would, for one reason or another, prefer you to dress in the dark. Make sure you keep to your own section of the hanging space, however. It avoids conflict, confusion and comment in the office. Separate full-length and half-length items within your own section. You might even try sub-dividing shirts and suits by colour, occasion or venue – office, evening, formal, informal, restaurant, club, very casual, resistible, irresistible, ski-slope, tennis court, golf course, sauna…

Socks and underwear are happy when horizontal but are easier to identify in the early hours if housed in separate compartments within drawer organizers or dividers. Place a tie rack over an otherwise empty closet door and your complete collection can be seen at a glance while remaining in good condition. Prune it from time to time or it may overflow. Attach hooks and pegs to redundant surfaces and hang belts, umbrellas and bags on them to make space work for you. Shoe racks will help you keep track of your footwear.

Don't cram small items such as belts and ties in the drawer if you lack space. Hang them on hooks or a special tie rack attached to the door. You will find them more easily in a hurry.

Open and shut case

Label drawers if you can't remember what's inside each one. If you share your closet with a partner this can help to avoid arguments about space encroachment. Be subtle – don't spray paint your name just to make a point. Graffiti is for walls.

SPACE ODYSSEY

Get close and personal
Closets, like people, benefit from being organized, orderly, logical and hard-working, both vertically and horizontally. Like you, they can become just the opposite. Trousers enjoy tall spaces. What they lose in unfortunate creases, you gain in sartorial stature.

Arms folded
Fold your woollens and sweaters carefully and store horizontally on narrow shelves. Put those for summer at the top when winter comes, and vice versa. Store by colour so that you can find the one you want quickly in the morning or when about to go on a date.

Keep space alive
Use dead space at the very top of the closet for suitcases and bags. Store boxes at the bottom with stuff inside them to make maximum use of space. Keep spares of things in your suitcase to save time when packing for an urgent business trip.

Open and shut
Keep socks and underwear in drawers. Again, don't just hurl them in when they are clean and dry. Use dividers to keep them in order – never store socks without their partner. It is just too cruel. Socks mate for life. That's nature – you have to respect that.

Collared
Always hang your shirts in the closet with enough space between them to avoid creasing. Otherwise, why bother ironing in the first place? Use proper hangers and remove stuff from jacket pockets before suspending. Don't leave clothes in their dry-cleaning bags.

DIY Sewing Skills

O k guys, now for some rather more delicate hands-on skills. No excuses, don't try the 'I'm all fingers and thumbs when it comes to detailed manual work' line. Fingers and thumbs are just what you need, plus a sewing survival kit. Read on to find out how to avoid finding yourself exposed to the elements, after a button goes absent without leave. A stitch in time saves nine, saves face, saves blushes and saves money. Surgeons use these skills all the time and everyone thinks they are wonderful. You'll soon have it sewn up.

First things first – the sewing survival kit. Keeping a mini kit on hand is an excellent and very practical idea. Put one in your briefcase for conferences and business trips. Pop a version in your rucksack for camping and backpacking holidays and always keep one in the car. A sewing kit is just a small-scale version of a tool kit so here are a few key items to keep in stock:

- Packet of needles of different lengths and sizes
- Pins (rust-proof preferably, with plain or plastic heads)
- Pincushion (not a fancy affair, just one that keeps pins in place)
- Safety pins (small and large)

- Thread (assorted colours, i.e. black, blue, white and brown)
- Needle threader
- All-purpose scissors (small enough to fit your kit)
- Assorted buttons (different sizes, colours, two- and four-hole)
- Tape measure
- Thimble (for those with a low pain threshold)

Remember, a bad workman always blames his tools so get the best quality kit and you'll be off to a good start. Imagine the following embarrassing scenario and you'll be glad to have the sewing skills:

HELP! MY BUTTON'S COME OFF AND EVERYONE CAN SEE MY CHEST!

Don't panic. Get out your sewing survival kit and set about fixing the problem. If you can't find the missing button itself, find a similar one or remove one from a less conspicuous place on the shirt.

Shirt off your back: only very experienced button-holers will be able to sew a button back on an item of clothing while still wearing it. You could puncture key parts of your anatomy, so do remove the garment before applying your new skills.

Make your mark: Using a pencil, mark where the button should go (i.e. its original, now empty, spot).

Colour co-ordination: choose a thread colour that matches or is slightly darker than the shirt fabric.

An eye for detail: thread your needle with a generous length (24 inches/61 cm) of medium thread, using the needle threader.

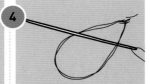

1 Tie a knot in it: tie a knot at the end of thread to keep it in place when you make your first stitch. When experienced, you can make one or two small stitches instead.

2 Button it: place the button in position (centred over the chosen spot). Insert the needle into one of the holes from the wrong side of the button and bring the needle up.

3 Looping: insert into the hole next to it, passing through from the right to the wrong side of the fabric. Repeat this process a few times, but don't make it too tight or you won't be able to do up the shirt.

4 Right and wrong: take the needle through to the wrong side of the fabric and secure by making a small stitch, inserting the needle through the loop and pulling tight. Repeat and cut.

20 THINGS A SMART MAN SHOULD KNOW:

CLOTHES CARE

1. Wash and dry clean garments only when they need it. This minimizes wear and tear and reduces bills.

2. When purchasing clothes, check the care label closely to avoid having too many items that are hand- wash or dry clean only.

3. Don't put dirty clothes back in the closet. Do you put dirty plates back in the cupboard? Don't answer that.

4. Air clothes after wearing them – lie woollen garments flat on the bed for an hour or so to dispel nasty odours such as smoke.

5. Invest in a clothes brush and lint tape roller to keep clothes free of hair, surface dirt and soil.

6. Brush clothes regularly and thoroughly. They will perk up quickly.

7. Apply new cologne before dressing to prevent impregnating clothes with an untried, unsuitable scent and avoid heavy cologne.

IRON KNOWLEDGE

8. A shot of steam removes wrinkles quickly and effectively. In the absence of a steamer, take your clothes into the shower room with you for a quick dose of the hot stuff.

9. Don't iron stained clothes – it will make the stains harder to remove.

CLOSET CLUES

10. Remove clothes from protective plastic bags as soon as you can – they promote light damage and mildew and can cause leather and suede to dry out.

11. Gradually replace your wire hangers with plastic, wooden or padded ones.

12. Dry damp or wet garments thoroughly before putting back in the closet.

13. Treat stains as soon as you can. Exposure to heat and light sets the stain and can make it impossible to budge.

14. Allow underarm deodorant to dry before putting on your clothes to avoid unsightly white stains.

15. Don't wear pins or badges on woollen garments. They will puncture your style

HANG ON IN THERE

16. Try not to hang a jacket or coat by the neck or on a coat hook or rack.

17. Allow suits to hang with enough space to air and lose their wrinkles before putting in the closet. Try using the door.

18. Take shoes to be re-soled or mended before holes appear and the rain comes in.

19. Give your shoes a rest – alternate a couple of pairs to keep them in shape longer.

20. If your zipper sticks, rub a lead pencil over it and things will run more smoothly in the trouser department.

Dress Sense

Think of your closet as an investment portfolio. Buy your clothes intelligently and sensibly with a view to long-term rewards and your quality purchases will bring dividends. Buying cheap clothes is a 'fast buck' strategy that can work with your more disposable items of attire. Remember to look after your long-term large investments though – your work clothes and shoes. For the rest, here's what to do:

A serious cull of your clothes always makes you feel good and leaves you with a fresh eye for fashion. Anything lurking within the closet that has not seen daylight for over a year must be a serious contender for the charity or recycling bin. Clothes that are much too small or too large for your physique need to go and you can also wave goodbye to items that need mending but are unlikely ever to see a needle and thread.

If you still lack closet space after a ruthless edit, divide clothes into winter and summer items and find a storage space for next season's range. Put clothes into vacuum-packed bags under the bed, in plastic lidded crates under the stairs or up in the loft. Ensure clothes are clean before you store them. When the next season dawns, apply the above principles of style and ruthlessness before giving them closet space. Always use proper hangers – ones that will not rust and have broad, supportive shoulders – they will extend the life of your clothes.

SUIT YOURSELF

JUST TO RECAP THE STRATEGY FOR PROLONGING THE LIFE OF YOUR SUITS AND PROTECTING YOUR INVESTMENT:

- PURCHASE TWO (OR, IF YOU CAN AFFORD IT, THREE) SUITS AND ALTERNATE THEM.
- BUY TWO PAIRS OF TROUSERS FOR EACH SUIT TO AVOID SHINY SEAT SYNDROME.
- SEND SUITS TO THE DRY-CLEANERS THREE OR FOUR TIMES A YEAR AND REMOVE THEM FROM PLASTIC PACKAGING THE MINUTE YOU GET THEM HOME.
- USE PROPER HANGERS AND HANG UP BOTH TROUSERS AND JACKET EVERY NIGHT WITH POCKETS EMPTIED, BELT REMOVED, BUTTONS AND ZIPS DONE UP.
- GIVE SUITS SPACE TO BREATHE IN THE CLOSET (AND IN THE SHOWER ROOM TO REMOVE WRINKLES QUICKLY).
- BRUSH AND AIR SUITS REGULARLY.
- REPAIR OR HAVE REPAIRED REGULARLY (A STITCH IN TIME SAVES NINETY-NINE LATER ON).
- AVOID (OR KEEP A VERY CLOSE EYE ON) PENS IN POCKETS – THEY EXPLODE OR LEAK REGULARLY.

X NO-NOS

Never wear belt and braces at the same time: it's one or the other. Your choice depends upon where you need support most.

Go easy on the flashy buckle unless you are auditioning for a bit part in a cowboy film: subtle is the way to go. Do you want everyone to stare at your waist?

White socks and dark shoes were not made for each other. Red socks are OK for special presentations (personal or professional) but white is out.

Make your own music, guys. A loud shirt is sometimes OK and a statement tie helps the conversation flow. Together though they don't strike the right note – ever.

FASHION FAUX PAS

Many women envy the fact that men can simply pull on suit, shirt and tie and rush out of the door in the morning without spending precious minutes deciding what to wear. However, here are some tips that you would do well to consider:

BELT AND SHOES
SHOULD MATCH – BLACK BELT AND BROWN SHOES DO NOT.

SHINY BOTTOMS
(ON TROUSERS) ARE A BIG NO-NO. BUY TWO PAIRS OF TROUSERS PER SUIT TO AVOID THIS. ALTERNATING TWO OR THREE SUITS HELPS EVEN MORE.

WHILE A BLACK SUIT
IS A RELIABLE CHOICE FOR MOST OCCASIONS – INTERVIEWS, PRESENTATIONS, BIRTHDAYS AND WEDDINGS – WEARING BLACK EVERY DAY IS NOT A GOOD LOOK. RING THE CHANGES BY WEARING A GREY OR BLUE SUIT FROM TIME TO TIME.

BLACK
CAN MAKE BIGGER MEN LOOK THINNER AND HIDES STAINS MORE SUCCESSFULLY.

IF YOUR SUIT JACKET
IS SOMEWHAT BAGGY OR OBVIOUSLY WRINKLY WHEN YOU BUTTON IT UP, YOU NEED TO BUY A NEW ONE – OR ELSE YOU HAVE PICKED UP SOMEONE ELSE'S BY MISTAKE IN THE GYM OR OFFICE.

SCRUFFY,
UNPOLISHED SHOES REFLECT SIMILAR TRAITS IN YOUR CHARACTER. YOU MAY THINK THAT 'PLEASE TAKE CARE OF ME' LOOK IS APPEALING. IT REALLY ISN'T.

DOUBLE-BREASTED
SUIT JACKETS SHOULD BE RESTRICTED TO SLIM RATHER THAN PORTLY FIGURES AND THOSE AIMING FOR A CLASSIC, MORE MATURE LOOK. SINGLE-BREASTED SUITS WORK FOR MOST SHAPES.

IF YOU ARE NOT AS TALL
AS YOU WOULD LIKE, A PINSTRIPE SUIT IS A GOOD CHOICE. IF YOU THINK YOU CAN ADD HEIGHT WITH OBVIOUS AND BULKY SHOULDER PADS, YOU ARE VERY MISTAKEN.

BUY AN
INTERESTING, EVEN SENSATIONAL, TIE EVERY YEAR. WEAR IT WHEN YOU WANT TO BE THE FOCUS OF CONVERSATION.

STEP-BY-STEP SARTORIAL STYLE

Look at your reflection in the mirror. Follow the instructions for a knot that's not half bad.

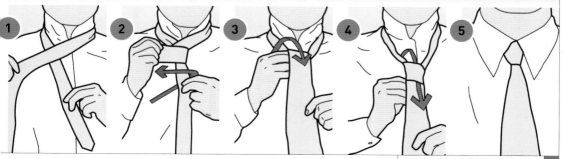

Domestic God in the Bedroom

R esearch shows people often judge one another by looking first at their shoes and then at their watch. Shoes are especially revealing and prospective partners may base their first and lasting impression of you on your footwear, so be warned. If we spend one third of our lives in bed, we must spend at least another third on our feet. Look after your shoes properly and they will last longer, look smarter and save you money.

DOMESTIC GOD A FEW TIPS

Keep in shape
Shoe trees keep leather shoes in shape and make them easier to clean and polish. Insert the trees before putting shoes away. Make your own boot trees with newspaper or cardboard. Use a shoehorn when putting shoes on in order to avoid crushing the backs. Untreated sandalwood horns absorb moisture from the leather, but you can use a metal spoon to ease your foot into your shoe if desperate. Loosen laces before removing shoes and use your hands to take shoes off – not your other shoe. Never tread on the heels.

Down at heel
Don't wear shoes day after day. It is not good for your feet or your shoes. If you find stylish, comfortable shoes that you really like, invest in two pairs.

Wrap it up
Put your best shoes in a shoe bag or store in the original cardboard box (identifying them in some way). Don't just throw them in the bottom of the closet.

Puddle tactics
Use a leather waterproof agent to prevent water staining your shoes during wet weather.

New kids on the block
Shop for shoes at the end of the day when your feet are at their largest. Try both shoes on (one foot is likely to be bigger than the other) and walk around to check they fit and are comfortable. Don't buy the wrong size shoes just because they are half-price and the last pair in the shop. It never works. You will spend more money on repairing blisters.

Air apparent
Air your shoes as regularly as you air your bed (i.e. every day). Leave them out (not in the bedroom or garden) overnight to breathe. Leather needs 24 hours to regain its shape. To combat foot odour, sprinkle some bicarbonate of soda in your shoes first and then let them breathe. Wear cotton socks.

Rainy days
If your shoes get wet in the rain, remove them as soon as you can and stuff them with newspaper. Allow shoes to dry naturally, not in front of the fire or on a radiator. Use saddle soap (look along the same shelf as the one with the shoe polish or wax) to condition when finally dry and then polish.

Tip-top tip
If the plastic tips come off your laces, dip the ends in some (borrowed) clear nail varnish or burn the ends to seal them.

Polishing up your act

OK, so polishing your shoes isn't as exciting as climbing Mount Everest or negotiating the Atlantic single-handed. However, this important mission can be accomplished while watching television, listening to your favourite music, doing karaoke or learning a foreign language. Some key equipment is required, and you should select and purchase the best. Polish your shoes at least twice a week, if you can, or once a week if you are very busy.

A bluffer's guide to buffing

For a mirror shine on your caps, dampen the corner of a dry cloth, place a small amount of polish on the corner and rub into the shoe or boot in tiny, repeated circles until a shine develops (some say spitting on the shoe during this process helps). Repeat several times. Use cotton wool to give final shine to the top coat. Admire reflection. Military folk call this bulling. Prepare to impress.

GUIDE TO THE PERFECT SHOESHINE

SHOESHINE KIT

- OLD NEWSPAPER (TO PROTECT CHOSEN WORK SURFACE, CARPET OR TABLE)
- SHOESHINE BRUSH
- SHOE POLISH BRUSH (OR TOOTHBRUSH)
- POLISHING CLOTH (OR OLD T-SHIRT)
- SHOE POLISH OR CREAM
- ELBOW GREASE

 **1**

1 Cover your intended work surface with an old newspaper and use a damp cloth to remove debris and dirt from your shoes. Don't use the shoe brush to do this or the dirt will transfer onto the brush. Dirt is the enemy of shine.

 **2**

2 Wipe shoes dry. Place a small amount of matching shoe polish on the tip of the shoe polish brush or toothbrush and spread evenly over the shoe. Take time out to let the polish sink in – why not iron a shirt, wash the bath or vacuum the living room?

 **3**

3 Using the shoeshine brush, brush polish away.

 **4**

4 Buff with a clean, lint-free cloth, rubbing vigorously.

See above for the encore that could lead to a glittering career. Quick march to success.

HELP BOX

 Q

Help! I've run out of polish and I've got a big meeting this morning!

 A

Use furniture polish or floor wax – just this once.

 Q

Help! Do I have to wear socks with my shoes?

A

Not with casual loafers but wearing no socks with your best dress shoes is a no-no. You will look as if you got dressed in the dark, in a hurry, or at someone else's place. Perhaps you did . . .

 Q

Help! I am so busy I have to choose between doing some exercise or polishing my shoes!

 **A**

Do both. Polishing your shoes vigorously, using serious elbow grease, could use up to 100 calories.

Domestic God's Routine (6pm to 9am)

O K, we've established that running a household is not unlike running a business. You've probably got the daytime routine more or less under your belt, but you may well be struggling with the best tactics for the evening agenda. The success of My Place Inc. relies on the same skills, demanding strategy, discipline, motivation and flair. It's now time to apply all of these to a different but just as important routine – one that underpins the smooth-running of the operation between 5pm and 9am. The goal: to learn, develop and expand the skills of the Domestic God. Business Tycoon/Big Success by day, Domestic God by night – different career ladder, same pinnacle of success, comparable job satisfaction and rewards. Remember snakes and ladders –you are happy climbing the ladder 9am-5pm, but don't slip back down after hours. Know the game, learn the rules, roll the dice and play to win.

DOMESTIC GOD THE OUT-OF-HOURS LIFE OF A DOMESTIC GOD

6pm ▷	6.15pm ▷	6.45pm ▷	8-10pm ▷	10pm ▷
ARRIVAL AT MY PLACE INC	**DEBRIEF**	**ADMINISTRATION AND REFRESHMENT**	**COMMUNICATION AND THE MEDIA**	**TYING UP LOOSE ENDS**
Greet partner, dog, cat, fish with cheery smile. Feed and water where appropriate, prepare chilled wine or hot, comforting beverage for partner, according to instructions, and then self. Check how partner's day has been and retire briefly to bedroom.	Remove daywear, exchange for casual outfit, hang up work clothes as necessary (see page 108), after emptying pockets, removing belt and placing money and keys in obvious place. Put shoe trees in shoes and store in wardrobe, after dealing with any offending odours (see page 114). Collate dirty clothes for laundry. Lie on bed, do physical and breathing exercises. Tidy room. Emerge refreshed and ready to assume multi-tasking evening role.	Deal with urgent bills, emails, phone messages. Fifteen minutes of PA per day keeps weekends free. Prepare simple, balanced, nourishing meal for self (and partner), demonstrating culinary skills and awareness of importance of healthy regime. Wash up dirty dishes and pans, tidy kitchen and wipe surfaces clean.	Relax in living area, engage with partner, sort joint and separate diaries, read papers, watch television, listen to radio or music. Get up to speed in personal, national and international affairs.	Iron clothes for next day for self and partner. Polish shoes. Tidy living area, plump cushions, remove old papers and debris, take trash out and wash up cups and glasses. Check pets'/ plants' needs.

Like any strategy, becoming a Domestic God (5pm-9am) involves careful planning. It doesn't just happen overnight. A step-by-step approach is key. Like any top job, it involves hard work and dedication. Let's take it hour by hour: You're spending an evening at home, in this case alone, with a partner and/or pets. Times are not set in stone and will vary according to length of working or study hours, journey etc. For some the commute may be only a few steps from the office to the kitchen. Whatever the case, it all starts when you get through the door into the kitchen. Deep breath, you're home.

10.40pm ▶

TIME AND MOTION
Check supplies and prepare shopping list. Take dirty clothes to utility room and programme for overnight wash. Fold clean, dry clothes and place in ironing basket. Place dry-cleaning near front door with briefcase Lock doors and check house and car keys are in obvious place. Prepare clothes for next day. Ask partner if there's anything you can do to help them get ready for tomorrow.

11pm ▶

RETIREMENT PROVISIONS
Prepare for bed, complete bathroom routine, relax in bath, listen to music, give bathroom a quick clean.

12-7am ▶

REST AND RECUPERATION
Open a window slightly, communicate or debrief with partner, sleep as soundly and noise-lessly as possible in order to recoup mental and physical energy for 9am-5pm agenda.

7am ▶

FAST TRACK OPERATION
Greet partner, air bed, pets. Execute early morning self-cleansing tasks, arrange breakfast for partner, self and pets, make bed, find keys, phone, diary and briefcase and enjoy smooth, stress-free exit.

8-9am ▶

DELIVERY
Arrive at place of work or study, calm and ready for daytime challenges. Deal with e-mails, phone messages and urgent memos. Diairize, prioritize, organize. 9am-5pm begins.

Guest Who's Coming to Stay

It always seems like such a good idea to invite parents, relatives or friends (yours or your partner's) to stay until the day approaches, and you become increasingly anxious. Treat the visit like an important presentation to a key client, potential employer or college lecturer. The product: My Place Inc. The target market: member(s) of A-list social circle. The strategy: to impress, welcome, win over and generally spoil. The time frame: one day or two evenings. The action plan: read, digest and implement the following advice, calmly:

HOW TO BE HOSPITABLE

- TRY TO FIND OUT WHEN GUESTS ARE PLANNING A VISIT. PRE-EMPT RATHER THEN PANIC BLINDLY.

- IF GUESTS ARRIVE ON A FRIDAY EVENING YOU CAN RELAX WITH THEM AHEAD OF A WHOLE DAY TOGETHER ON SATURDAY AND HOPEFULLY THEY WILL LEAVE AFTER LUNCH ON SUNDAY.

- SAY 'HELLO AND WELCOME' WITH A GLASS OF CHILLED WINE OR FIZZ. THEY WILL FEEL SPECIAL. IF THEY ARE NOT, BUY FAKE CHAMPAGNE OR BEER.

- ARRANGE AN OUTING – A VISIT TO A LOCAL MUSEUM, MARKET OR LANDMARK WILL DO. CHECK OUT FIRST IF HISTORY, GEOLOGY OR SHOPPING IS THEIR HOBBY.

- ORGANIZE A RELAXING WALK THAT LEADS TO A CHARMING WATERING HOLE. OFFER TO PAY FOR THE FIRST ROUND, EXPECT NOT TO HAVE TO.

- IF IT'S A CHILLY NIGHT, LIGHT A FIRE IN THE LIVING ROOM (SEE PAGE 66). IF IT'S HIGH SUMMER, HAVE THE BARBECUE READY. WARMTH COMES IN ALL FORMS.

- RESEARCH THEIR EATING HABITS. A MEAT FEST WON'T GO DOWN WELL WITH VEGETARIANS.

- IF THEY OFFER TO COOK A MEAL, ACCEPT. IT WILL MAKE THEM FEEL AT HOME. THEIR CULINARY SKILLS MIGHT OUT-DO YOURS.

- SPRAY SOME LAVENDER SCENT IN THEIR BEDROOM AT NIGHT – THEY WILL BE ASLEEP IN NO TIME.

DON'T SAY YES TO NO-NO'S

Banish no-nos from the living area (page 57), dining room (page 79), bedroom (page 103), kitchen (page 15) and bathroom (page 125). If the utility area and your office are not looking at their best, keep guests out. Whatever part of the cleaning operation you miss, it will be discovered. Prepare for constructive criticism of your proposal.

DON'T PANIC

Remember, your guest wants to see and spend time with you rather than inspect where you live. If tidiness involves extra temporary storage, then go for it but promise yourself you will sort it out as soon as your guest has gone. If time is short, focus your cleaning activity on the obvious areas of the most important rooms: kitchen and bathroom surfaces are top of the list, washing the curtains and walls are not. For specific operations, check the relevant pages of this book. Enjoy playing host and the 'welcoming' part of the strategy will come naturally.

WELCOME TO MY PLACE INC.

Clean and clear the guest room. Remove any inappropriate reading matter from previous occupants, tidy, dust, wipe and vacuum. Ensure sheets are clean and wrinkle-free. Add a few luxuries such as a vase of flowers, a glossy magazine (check tastes first), fresh fruit or biscuits, sweet-smelling soaps and a fresh fluffy towel on the bed. Turn back the bed covers at night, check the room temperature and always let your guest use the bathroom first. Prepare a tasty but healthy breakfast the next day after delivering a cup of tea to the room.

HELP! MY PARTNER'S MUM IS IN TOWN UNEXPECTEDLY AND WANTS TO COME AND STAY. THE HOUSE IS A MESS. WE'VE GOT TWO HOURS. WHAT SHALL WE DO?

Put sheets on short cycle wash and dry. Find clean towel. Take two rooms each (kitchen, living area, bathroom and guest's bedroom). Execute emergency tidy, dusting and wiping operation. Vacuum each room plus entry hall. Spray furniture polish in living area. Plump cushions. Clean bath and toilet. Put dirty laundry in utility room. Use room sprays for a fragrant welcome. Put out the trash and clean the bin. Place beer cans at back of fridge and fresh items to the front. Open door and greet guest with relaxed smile.

Suitcase Savvy

I f you're hopeless at packing and always seem to arrive at the airport like a bad-tempered beast of burden while everyone else has smart, compact luggage and a smug smile, no worries. Buy a lightweight suitcase and follow these tips:

THINK OF A NUMBER AND HALVE IT

Put out all the clothes you plan to take with you on your bed and divide them into piles of underwear, socks, shirts, T-shirts, trousers and jeans, shoes and sneakers, sweaters etc. Now halve each one, except for the underwear pile. This is the amount you really need.

Dark-coloured clothes are practical, since minor stains will be less obvious, but they're less suitable for very hot destinations. For chilly or unpredictable climates, opt for the 'layer upon layer' strategy rather than taking bulky sweaters. Wear your bulkiest footwear and jacket for travelling to save space and weight in the case.

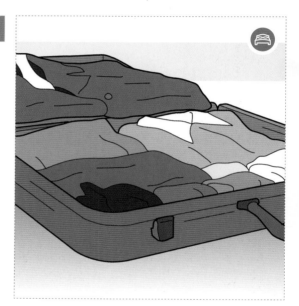

DON'T SAY YES TO NO-NO'S

Pack your heaviest items (shoes, books and toiletry kits) along the spine of the suitcase. Place folded socks, underwear and rolled up belts in your shoes. Put shoes in individual protective bags (for extra flexibility) or wrap with tissue or plastic to avoid soiling neighbouring clothes with debris or polish. Take miniatures of your toiletries if possible. Decant shampoos and other potions into small plastic bottles then wrap them in plastic bags to avoid leakage.

HELP!

My suit is full of wrinkles and I've got a big interview first thing tomorrow!
Look for the trouser press and instructions or call room service.

DOMESTIC GOD'S
CHECK CHECK CHECK

Have on board, ready for take off:

- An empty soft bag for purchases, souvenirs and presents for partner
- Laundry bag for dirty linen.
- Voltage converter or adaptor for electrical appliances.
- Visible piece of paper with your details and contact information at destination placed on top of your clothes.
- A complete pharmacy is not required – buy on arrival if necessary. Stick to the basics, such as shampoo, deodorant, cologne, toothpaste, toothbrush, sunscreen, insect repellent and contact lens equipment.
- A piece of bright, even garish fabric tied to your luggage as identification for the carousel.
- Locks and relevant keys.

Don't leave home without...

- Documents, tickets, schedule and passport.
- Emergency contact numbers (for lost credit cards etc).
- Spare pair of contact lenses and a pair of prescription glasses.
- Medication (plus spare prescription using drug's generic name).
- Combination for locks (if you can't keep it in your head).
- Computer
- Camera
- Phone
- Calculator

SUIT YOURSELF

Some people like to use suit bags when they travel. There's no folding involved and you can take your proper hangers with you. To pack a suit, first fold the jacket sleeves over the back and then fold the jacket in half. Turning the jacket inside out before folding is an option. Trousers can be folded and packed in a number of ways. One method is to line the bottom of your suitcase with a pair of trousers, creases in place, leaving the legs to dangle over the edge. Pack the rest of your clothes on top, lighter garments last, and then fold the trouser legs over the pile. This keeps the crease intact. Alternatively, fold trousers neatly in three, aligning inner and outer leg seams first so that you get a proper crease at the front. Fold jeans in half and then roll to fit in a sneaky space.

GET SHIRTY

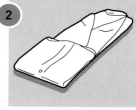

Shirts should be neatly folded and packed at the top of the case to avoid crushing. Always place flat items over bulky clothes. Pack some good hangers too as hotel ones are often very flimsy. Use space cleverly and allow clothes some breathing space. Place breakables in bubble wrap and pack them between soft items.

BATHROOM

Hygiene Harmony
A sparkling sink is important for hygiene, health and household harmony.

Keep it Clean
Clean the toilet every day.

Polish Up
Polish your mirrors every week to reflect Domestic God status.

'YOU LEARN MORE ABOUT A MAN FROM
HIS BATHROOM THAN HIS BEDROOM.'

Joanna Rampley-Sturgeon

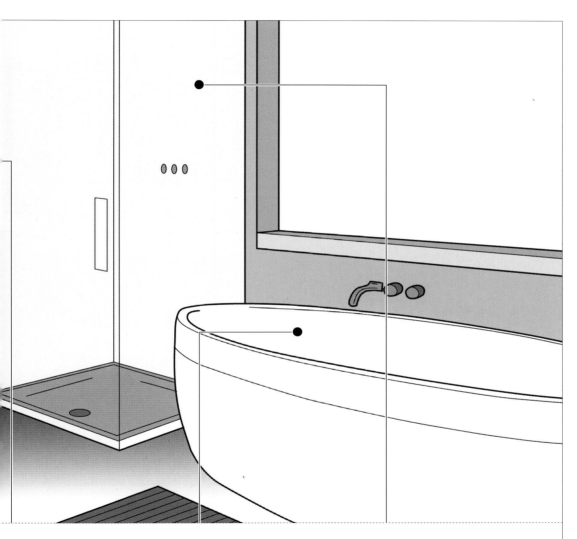

Stock Up
Keep important bathroom supplies
in stock.

Tidemarks
After bathing, clean your bath to
avoid unsightly tidemarks.

No Mould
Clean your shower curtain
regularly to keep mould at bay.

In the Bathroom

T he smallest room in the house is one of the most intimate. For guests and partners (existing and potential), the bathroom is a window on your personal hygiene, a kind of waterproof stage on which you strut your stuff. So keep it clean, guys. The only lines in there should be the ones you sing or rehearse – not the ones you leave behind in the bath. There is nothing nastier than the sight of a previous bather's tidemark, except for a sink full of stubble, so make the bathroom a sanctuary, a haven, a place in which you and your partner or guests can feel restored. If you emerge feeling dirtier than when you went in, something is wrong.

Here are a few no-nos to help you hitch a ride on the highway to hygiene heaven.

CHORE CHART: WHAT TO DO WHEN

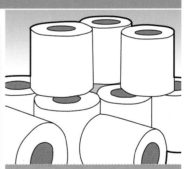

DAILY:
- CLEAN TOILET AND SINK
- CHECK SUPPLIES
- TRASH THE TRASH
- REPLACE TOILET PAPER
- REMOVE DIRTY LAUNDRY

WEEKLY:
- CLEAN BATH (TWICE A WEEK)
- CHANGE BATH TOWELS (DITTO)
- CLEAN UNIT TOPS
- WASH BATHMAT
- POLISH MIRROR
- VACUUM OR SWEEP FLOOR

MONTHLY:
- CLEAN FLOOR THOROUGHLY
- POLISH TAPS
- CHECK SUPPLIES OF TOILET PAPER, SHAMPOO AND SOAP
- CLEAN SHOWER CURTAIN (EVERY TWO MONTHS)
- MAKE INVENTORY OF MEDICINE CABINET CONTENTS
- WASH PAINTWORK AND TILES

X NO-NOS

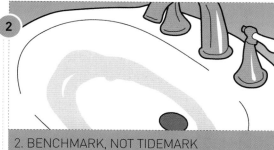

1. UP IS A DOWNER

Leaving the toilet seat up is a habit that most of the male population indulge in. It may be a cliché, but it's so true, so make sure it's a definite no-no in the smallest room in the house. However practical it may be (no explanations required) it is not uplifting for others. It gives out too much information on what is after all a very personal activity in a highly private space. An intimate act should remain just that, with no circumstantial evidence. Respect the seating arrangements in the bathroom just as you do in the dining room.

2. BENCHMARK, NOT TIDEMARK

Devise and adhere to a bathroom routine that takes less than five minutes to complete yet saves you hours of anguish and work. One excellent preventative measure is to use bath or shower gel every time you run a bath – this reduces the likelihood or intensity of the tidemark and you'll come out of it smelling sweet. Clean the bath and the sink as soon as you can after use – the later you leave it, the longer it takes. Do it now, save a row. A bit of cream cleanser on a cloth, a touch of elbow grease.

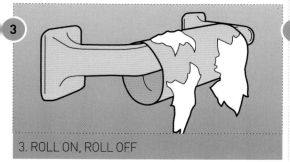

3. ROLL ON, ROLL OFF

Ancient man may have made do with leaves and grass, modern man in extremis may resort to substitutes, but for the most part we prefer the stationery in the bathroom to be nice, soft toilet paper. Like waves in the ocean, when one roll has gone, another follows in its wake, not far behind. It's up to you to keep up this natural momentum. Replace one roll with another without leaving a hiatus. You don't want to embarrass guests or new friends, do you? Keep plentiful supplies of the stuff, with a replacement roll always on hand. Use an attractive basket to store them (not a crochet cover from your aunty).

4. OLD NEWS IS BAD NEWS

You may like to catch up on the latest news in the smallest room but don't leave papers, magazines and nasty joke books strewn over the floor and surfaces, creating unnecessary clutter in a room intended for the three Rs. This is where you refresh, relax and restore. Take old news with you and recycle it. A bathroom can get hot and steamy and the last thing you need is damp, smelly, yellowing paper, curling at the edges as if embarrassed to be there. It isn't a library, after all. If you must treat it as a reading room, keep your literature (if it can be called that) in a neat pile or in a basket.

Domestic God: Top-to-Toe Hygiene

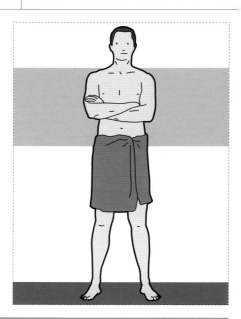

T here is no point making a valiant effort to keep your home in order if you fail to pay similar attention to your body. Is it not a temple after all? However attractive, impressive and strangely seductive a squeaky clean kitchen, sparkling bathroom or immaculate bedroom may be, ignoring personal hygiene will deter partners, friends and even relatives – big time. If you want to be a groom, do the grooming. It's that simple. Think of parts or areas of your physique as rooms in your home, requiring different degrees of tidiness and cleanliness. Let's take it from the top.

DOMESTIC GOD TOP-TO-TOE HYGIENE ROUTINE

Hair ▷	Eyebrows ▷	Eyes ▷	Face ▷	Nose & Ears ▷
Shampoo and condition regularly – it takes five minutes in the shower. Choose a product that suits your hair type and if you suffer from dandruff, use a shampoo that combats the problem. Dandruff is dead skin cells mixed with oil and dirt – it sounds unpleasant and looks worse. Have regular haircuts and listen to others on the subject of ponytails, mullets, shaven heads or hair accessories.	Ask your barber, hairdresser or partner to trim and control these for you. Don't ask an ex-partner, or you may find one missing.	Your eyes are the windows to your soul and reflect your habits, particularly the nocturnal ones. Get as much sleep as your body needs rather than as little as your self-imposed routine allows. Eat and drink alcohol in sensible moderation, but drink lots of water to keep hydrated. Reduce puffiness with slices of cucumber. Red equals stop. Don't choose it for your eyes or you will never get the green light in romance.	Wash your face morning and night with soap, gel or cleanser. If you have sensitive skin, find a gentle product that suits you. Pay attention to the T-zone (forehead and nose) where skin can be oily and prone to pimples. Remember this is the face you will have for years to come. Wear sunscreen unless you like the craggy look. Exfoliate regularly and moisturize daily. Lotions and potions are not just for girls.	Perversely, hair seems to emigrate from the top of your head and sprout in your nose and ears. Try to keep it under control with nose and hair groomers. Don't use tweezers (ouch) or scissors. Wash in and behind ears regularly and check nose for stalagmites or stalactites, particularly before meeting your new boss or mystery date.

Teeth ▷

Fresh breath, a nice smile and a bacteria-free mouth – aim for all three. Brush your teeth morning and night and in between if you can to remove food particles and plaque. Use mouthwash and mouth fresheners to remove unpleasant food odours. However romantic your words, spinach on your teeth will spoil the atmosphere. Replace your toothbrush every six to eight weeks or as soon as it looks down in the mouth.

Chin area ▷

Moisturize with balm after shaving to keep your skin smooth and supple. Designer stubble or a beard can be attractive but you might want to take advice on whether it's right for you. You will have to grow it to over 6 metres (18 feet) in length to have the longest beard in the world, by the way. A little splash of eau de cologne is more effective than a good drenching of it.

Lips ▷

Now you're talking. Keep them soft with lip balm (not gloss) or good old petroleum jelly. There are already more than enough toads around to kiss – don't be another statistic.

Upper torso ▷

Keep it clean, toned and moisturized. Skin is the largest organ you have – it protects you from all sorts of nastiness and deserves respect. Exercise strengthens the immune system, so a few stretches and sit-ups and a bit of jogging and general jiggling about will keep you fit and happy. Shower after exercise if you want to have a social life.

Armpits ▷

Regular washing and application of deodorant is the key to maintaining this area. Remember, you have over two million sweat glands. You may want to occasionally trim the region to keep perspiration under control – take care when you do and carry out the process in the shower, not the bedroom. Take some deodorant wipes with you to work or college if you have a big day ahead and a date at the end of it.

Stomach ▷

Keep your six-pack toned, clean and smooth, and your stomach button free of accumulated fluff. It is not a storage solution. No need to dust or vacuum, just wash.

Towel zone ▷

This T-zone must be kept impeccably clean and dry at all times. A large percentage of those sweat glands operate in this area. It's a hygiene-heavy district. Don't share towels at the gym. Change your underwear at least seven times a week.

Hands ▷

Wash thoroughly and often. Keep soft and supple with hand cream. Make holding hands fun and sensual. Brush nails every day. Dirty fingernails are a no-no and long ones can be a real turn-off, so trim them weekly.

Legs ▷

Wash, moisturise and exercise regularly. You rely on them to get you from A to B. If they send out an SOS, a calf massage in a warm bath will help.

Feet ▷

You can get Athlete's Foot even if the only action you see is on television. Foot fungus loves dark and damp conditions, so keep your feet clean and dry and use an anti-fungal product if they become itchy or smelly. Change your socks every day and take them off at bedtime. Rub your heels with a pumice stone in the bath to make them look and feel smooth. Use peppermint foot lotion to keep odours at bay.

Keep it Clean

Bathroom hygiene is of paramount importance but needn't be too taxing on muscles or patience. If you do no cleaning, you will create the perfect conditions for an experiment in bacterial reproduction. Generally speaking, bathrooms are humid environments in which mould and mildew party so open the windows, keep the room warm and dry and hang up your dirty, wet towels.

MIRROR ON THE WALL

Use a clean cloth dipped in a solution of water with a hint of vinegar and polish with a newspaper for an old-fashioned gleam.

If you prefer the more modern approach, use a glass cleaner spray but spray the cloth rather than the mirror and work from the middle outwards. That way the liquid won't run around the edges, causing the silver to oxidize and turn black. Once polished to perfection, admire your reflection.

BEAT THE BATHROOM BLUES

YOUR BATHROOM SHOULD BE EQUIPPED WITH:

- TIDY, CLEAN CUPBOARDS AND DRAWERS FOR COSMETICS, HAIR AND SHAVING EQUIPMENT, TOILET PAPER, CLEAN TOWELS ETC.
- CLEVER AND SAFE STORAGE FOR SMALLER CLEANING SUPPLIES AND TOOLS (LARGER ONES SHOULD LIVE IN THE UTILITY ROOM).
- A CHILDPROOF MEDICINE CABINET.
- A HEATED TOWEL RAIL.
- A LAUNDRY BAG OR BASKET.
- AN ARRAY OF HOOKS.

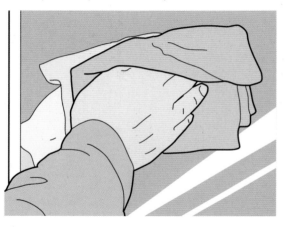

HELP!

Q Help! My partner says I have a body odour problem but I wash every day. What should I do?

A If you have a shower or bath every day but don't change your clothes, yesterday's body odour will linger (and the smells from the day before and the day before that...)

Q Help! My partner says I have to choose a new aftershave or a new address. Which one shall I go for?

A Decide which one makes your head swoon and go for that.

Q Help! I've heard that if you leave dirty clothes on the floor of your bedroom, they will eventually deodorize. Does this mean I can lie in bed for a couple of days without washing and get clean?

A Worth a try – but who will you ask whether you smell nice?

DOMESTIC GOD

Pull your weight in the bathroom, you know it's worth it.

Bathing was an important activity for the Romans and they sure had the right idea about it. Their public baths were multi-media entertainment centres for clean folk boasting libraries, gardens, walkways, balconies for sunbathing, theatres for poetry readings and music as well as a wide range of cleansing opportunities. For many of us today, relaxing in the bath continues to be one of life's great pleasures.

If, however, at the end of a hard day we are greeted by a dirty tub with an obvious and nasty ring around it, the pleasure of bathtime is somewhat diminished. Don't just close your eyes and climb in. Give it a good clean using a cloth and an appropriate non-abrasive cleaner – dishwashing liquid will dissolve stubborn residue. If you run out of commercial products or simply prefer to make your own, use a paste of bicarbonate of soda and water on a damp cloth and apply with elbow grease. Listen to the radio as you do this or practise your speech for the following day at the office. Your voice will sound encouragingly impressive. Rinse the bath thoroughly. Always use different cloths and sponges for the bath, toilet and walls or you will cross-contaminate. Keep them clean by giving them a regular wash in the machine, using hot water or by soaking in a solution of bleach and water. Grey, crusty cloths that lurk on the floor must be banished from the bathroom.

Naked housework

Why not try a spot of nude housework? Not as kinky as it sounds, it's quite a practical way of keeping your shower clean. Climb in and do the job in your birthday suit. Give the tiles and glass screens a wipe down using a sponge and a commercial tile and glass cleaner or use convenient bathroom wipes. You could try a spot of DIY by using a spray bottle filled with white vinegar. This will help keep limescale at bay. Spray on the surface, leave for a few minutes, rinse off and buff (in the buff). For all these substances, avoid contact with the skin. Emerge from the shower in reverse as you tackle the floor with a more robust, non-abrasive creamy cleaner. Rinse well. You could now climb back in and give yourself a wash down. Sing as you clean to release important feel-good hormones.

If you have a plastic shower curtain, keep it clean or it will go mouldy. Sponge it with water and bicarbonate of soda or put in the washing machine with some old, colourfast towels. Put on a warm wash but don't spin. Hang the curtain immediately. Chrome taps and showerheads can be washed with non-abrasive bathroom cleaners or a soft cloth dipped in white vinegar. Dry and buff (not in the buff this time, necessarily).

Out with the grout

A cleaner containing bleach will help tackle unattractive discoloration in your grouting. Use an old nailbrush or toothbrush to clean it but don't splash the cleaner on the carpet, curtains or yourself.

Sinks

Clean your porcelain sink with a creamy non-abrasive cleaner (or bathroom wipes). Once a surface becomes cracked, germs move in. Rinse the clean sink and dry thoroughly. It will look shiny and lovely – perfect for your guest. Stainless steel stinks can be washed with a dishwashing detergent. Rinse and dry. Avoid harsh abrasive cleansers.

Bidets

More and more bathrooms boast bidets nowadays. Once you have worked out how to use your particular model, make sure you keep it clean. Treat your bidet as you would your bath or sink.

Toilet Tactics: Flushed with Success

T oilets are made of strong stuff – they have to be. Theirs is one of the toughest jobs in the house. They are front line operatives and deserve respect. Neglect them at your peril. Germs, odours and other unwanted side effects will follow. If you have noticed that friends never use your bathroom, ask yourself why. It may be a No-Go area for reasons of hygiene rather then privacy. Think safety, cleanliness and appeal – toilets need them all. Keep it sparklingly clean, inside and out. Wash its exterior using the same method and products as for your bath, sink or bidet. You should disinfect the pan – choose from the many toilet cleaners available commercially but try not to splash the liquid, gel or powder as they may contain powerful chemicals. Lift toilet seat and, using your toilet brush, give the whole bowl a good scrub, under the rim and as far into the base as you can go. Rinse both bowl and brush by flushing and replace toilet seat. Wipe this clean with a separate, clean cloth and all-purpose cleaner. Replace lid. Always wash your hands afterwards and put a small amount of disinfectant in the toilet brush container, too.

UNBLOCKING A TOILET – SORTING A SLUGGISH FLUSH

1 Toilets can get blocked – it happens. So here's how to deal with it. Take a large long-handled open-flange plunger (hire one if necessary) and place over the drain opening at the base of the bowl, having bailed out excess water. Leave enough to cover the plunger cup. Pump up and down with vim and vigour (about 10 times), finishing with a final flourish (if not flush).

2 To find out if the flush holes in the rim are fully open, hold a mirror under the toilet bowl rim at an angle that allows you to see the holes. If you borrow your partner's mirror, make sure you wash it thoroughly afterwards or it will reflect badly on you.

3 To unblock rim flush holes, cut a short section of wire from a coat hanger and insert carefully in each hole, taking care not to damage the porcelain. Turn the wire to loosen mineral deposits that may have built up there.

4 If this tactic fails, you may want to hire a WC auger – a flexible rod with a crank handle at one end. The flexible part goes into the trap and you need to crank the handle with care (usually clockwise, but check instructions) to dislodge the pesky blockage.

TOILET TECHNIQUES

FLOOR STYLE

Always pick up your wet towel and hang it up to dry. Wash your towel regularly, and well before it develops an unpleasant, stale odour. Don't leave clothes strewn over the floor. Work out their itinerary and transport them to ultimate destination, whether laundry bag, wardrobe or utility room. Put bathroom mats in the wash every week, too.

TOP TOILET TIP

Borrow (permanently) a couple of denture-cleaning tablets from your grandparents and pop them into the toilet. Leave them overnight to do their thing and then brush and flush. Smile.

ODOUR EATER

Light a match to banish unwanted odours. This really works. Blow out match and place in bin. Whilst on the subject, don't smoke in the bathroom. Ever.

HAIR TODAY

Wash your combs and brushes regularly – twice a month if possible. They may look fine, but natural oils from your hair and shampoo residues build up on your hair care products as well as on your scalp. Wash in warm water and mild detergent and rinse well (your comb, not your scalp).

HOME AND AWAY HYGIENE

An old, dirty travelling wash bag is a no-no. When visiting friends, don't empty its nasty contents all over their clean bathroom surfaces, particularly if you have a soap container that looks more like a Petri dish and a toothbrush that looks as if it has seen some serious action. Buy a travel set of toiletries and tools and keep them clean and contemporary.

CLEAN TOILET, GIVE ME FIVE

5 minutes spent, 50 calories burned, 5 million germs zapped.

THE DRAIN GAME

To combat smelly drains without using bleach, try flushing boiling water and a handful of salt down the drain. Congealed grease will be dissolved.

The DIY Spa

After all your industrious household management, you deserve a spot of pampering and an opportunity to relax. Add a dash of imagination and a splash of oils to your bathroom and you can transform it into a home spa. No need to spend lots of money going to a health club; DIY luxury is the answer. Take time out and put life back on track, all within your own four walls. Keep the air circulating – open the windows as often and as wide as you can – and keep the room warm and dry. Dirty, wet towels on the floor will not help achieve this atmosphere and may create an entirely different one between you and any long-suffering housemates.

Choose a time that suits your partner or other housemates because you will be taking over the bathroom for several hours. If alone in the house, turn off all telephones and televisions. If not, hang a Please Do Not Disturb sign on the door of the bathroom. Take some water with you – you will have to keep hydrated – and some or all of the following:

- RELAXING MOOD MUSIC AND BATTERY-OPERATED CD PLAYER OR DOCKED MP3 PLAYER POSITIONED NEARBY
- SCENTED CANDLES
- A FEW ESSENTIAL OILS
- A CLEAN TOWEL
- A GLASS OF FRESHLY-SQUEEZED JUICE OR A STRESS-BUSTING SMOOTHIE (TRY BANANA WITH COCONUT MILK) AND/OR A BEER
- A PEELED, MASHED AVOCADO
- A JAR OF HONEY
- A SPOON
- A FACE SCRUB (COMMERCIAL OR NATURAL, I.E. STRAWBERRIES, PINEAPPLES, BANANAS)

PREPARE TO BE PAMPERED

You are about to enjoy some 'Domestic God Me Time'. You may feel inclined to lock the door – that's entirely your decision – but remember that a back massage from your partner might be a good way to end your spa.

Set the scene
Turn off the lights and let the candles illuminate the scene as the bath fills with warm water. Select music and play (gently does it). Pour six to eight drops of essential oil (lavender, bergamot and camomile are particularly calming) into the water. Different oils have different effects so a little pre-purchase research is worth the effort. The steam and warmth evaporate the oils and give off a wonderful aroma while softening your skin. You will feel uplifted as well as relaxed, soothed as well as restored. Choose an essential oil with a scent that appeals, add a few drops into a pump spray and dilute with water to make your own air freshener. It's that easy. If you feel awkward shopping for such 'pampering' items, pretend the oils are for your mother, or opt for a more anonymous on-line shopping experience.

Gadgets
There are numerous gadgets around that increase the relaxation factor once you are immersed. An inflatable waterproof pillow, a machine that transforms the bath into a whirling Jacuzzi, a foot spa and a battery-powered massager are just a few of the items that can create an out-of-this-world, out-of-water experience. None of these are as essential as the oils though – the warm water, the oils and the opportunity to debrief are highly effective in their own right.

Toe nails
Now that you're relaxed and refreshed, it is time to cut the toe nails (see page 127) and give yourself a foot scrub with a brush or pumice stone. Read a magazine or meditate. Think nice thoughts. Out with hate, in with love.

Conditioning
To condition the skin, mix pre-mashed avocado with a teaspoon of honey (you can do this in the bath) and apply liberally to your face as a mask, avoiding the eye area. Relax for 15 minutes and then rinse off with warm water. Nobody needs to know you've been dousing yourself with vegetation in the name of body maintenance. While you are at it, you could consider rubbing mashed banana on

to your hair to condition it the natural way. Rinse well before using conventional shampoo.

Exercise
Indulge in some bath exercises to improve muscle tone, but remember not to get your toe stuck in the tap. Don't laugh – it does happen. Stretch your legs, massage them gently and tense buttock muscles. Moisturize your body after a bath, while your skin is warm and absorbent.

DOMESTIC GOD
Having enjoyed a relaxing spa bath, prepare one for your partner. Do the housework, take the calls and share the pleasure while they enjoy.

DOMESTIC GOD'S TIPS FOR TOP-TO-TOE RELAXATION

Getting clean can be fun and relaxing. Enjoy the experience and experiment with ways of increasing the pleasure factor. Here are some cheap and cheerful ways.

HEAD MASSAGE

Sit up in the bath, relax your neck and close your eyes. Imagine your head is suspended from above. Breathe in deeply and exhale slowly, emptying your lungs. Count ten deep breaths in this way, keeping your head and neck relaxed. Open your eyes, think about something nice, and smile. Life feels good.

VEG OUT

Placing a slice of cucumber on each eye is both relaxing and refreshing. Hey, who's watching? Lemon juice can be used to soften the skin and cleanse stained hands. Tomatoes moisturize and act as good toners, while aloe vera soothes and nourishes your skin. Buy an aloe vera plant, cut off a stem then squeeze the juice directly onto the skin.

DO REAL MEN EXFOLIATE?

Even a rhinoceros exfoliates, so if it's good enough for such a majestic animal to wallow in mud, it's good enough for you. For as long as time itself, sand, ash and salt have been used by humans as an important pampering medium. Strawberries, pineapples and bananas make excellent natural exfoliators and rubbing avocado peel on your face is a good way of removing dead skin cells. If this all sounds a bit fruity, use a commercial face scrub. Your face will feel as smooth as a baby's bottom.

PUT YOUR FOOT IN IT

While a long bare-footed stroll on a sandy beach is the best way to exfoliate your feet, peppermint lotion is excellent for freshening up odorous extremities. And in the absence of the ocean, some mashed banana with a teaspoon of honey and a dash of lime juice is a good homemade alternative. If you're feeling fruity, spread it all over your feet, don a pair of cotton socks and keep them on overnight. You will awake feeling bananas and fleet of foot.

DO IT LIKE CLEOPATRA

For a truly Roman experience, pour some fresh organic milk in to the bath – pretend it is full of breakfast cereal and use enough for about three bowlfuls. Antony certainly seemed to like it. If you're in the mood for more of a cocktail soak, add coconut milk, yoghurt and honey (around a tablespoon of each) and a mashed banana. Relax – you'll eat your words.

RELAX STANDING UP

If you like a bit of suffering, rub your body with dead sea salt as you shower (ordinary sea salt will do if you run out). Leave on for a few minutes, rinse off and dry yourself with fluffy warm towels. It feels like a long swim in the ocean. Moisturize all over and do some gentle exercise.

STUBBLE TROUBLE

If things cut up rough on the chin front try an oil that has aloe vera, peppermint, tea tree oil or vitamin E in it. Find one that has all four and you'll smile from ear to ear.

TAKE CARE WITH HAIR

Don't use shower or bath gel to wash your hair. Stick to shampoo. Shower gel often contains powerful detergents and usually a good dose of fragrance, both of which could damage your hair. Interestingly, beer is good for hair (externally applied, of course).

GRIME STOPPERS Q AND A

 Q — **A** — **Q** — **A** — **Q** — **A**

Q: Why should I wash? Animals stay clean and they don't have bathtubs.

A: They may not use soap, but they are very resourceful. Zebras roll around in the dirt to get clean, thereby effectively removing dead skin and bugs. Ever smelt a zebra's armpit? Who needs to? Chimps ask close friends to pick out the bugs and dirt from their fur. Cats lick themselves clean (you could try that).

Q: I don't have many baths because I like to save water. My partner is complaining. What should I do?

A: Showers use less water than baths – enjoy a good soapy clean in just under three minutes. Time yourself and put an alarm clock in the bathroom to avoid wasting water. Install a water-saving showerhead. Well done on the ecological front – more work needed on personal hygiene.

Q: My partner would like us to bathe together in olive oil. What should I do?

A: Vegetable-based soaps are excellent and widely available, including olive oil soap. You can add a few drops of olive oil along with your essential oils to the bath water to moisturize your skin.

TAKE IT EASY – CREATE A COMPANY

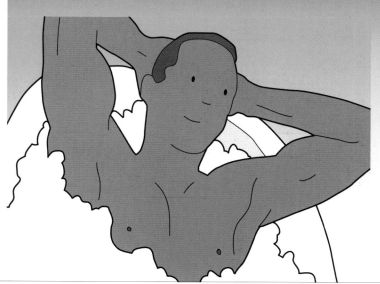

Let's face it guys – getting soaked isn't always a bad thing. After a hard day at the office, chilling out in a hot tub is a good way to unwind. Some of the best inventions and discoveries happened in the bath. Remember Archimedes? Just lie back and relax, let the oils or suds do their thing and eureka – a great business concept or idea for a thesis will come to you. Keep a pen and paper handy to scribble down your business model.

First Aid Kit

Every household should have a first-aid kit or a simply-equipped medicine cabinet. It doesn't have to be a mini pharmacy, but should consist of a basic kit to deal with minor accidents and common illnesses such as sore throats and headaches. Always make sure that you keep the supplies somewhere safe, preferably in a locked cupboard, high up, so that curious small folk cannot get to them.

If you already have a kit, now is the time to check it out. Uh oh. It's rather like your fridge used to be before you took advice – full of items with lost identities, some of them from distant shores. Remember that horrid tummy bug you had last year on holiday? Spot any sad-looking tubes from a bygone era? What about half-completed courses of medication? And what was that pink stuff encrusted on the bottle? Yuk. It's time to employ the 4Rs:

The 4 Rs
Review (the contents), **read** (the labels), **remove** (the culprits) and **restock** (with fresh supplies).

No, no, no, no, no!
- If you can't identify a medicine, throw it away instantly and safely.
- If a medicine has been prescribed for someone else's complaint, never take it yourself.
- Always finish a prescribed course of medicine (e.g. antibiotics) and dispose of the leftovers safely (you can take them back to the pharmacy if you are unsure).
- Don't keep medicines beyond their use-by dates. They may become harmful and they will certainly lose their effect.
- Don't leave medication lying around – keep it safely stored at all times and check that bottles have childproof lids.

Hangovers
Hangovers deserve individual treatment. Your head is throbbing, the room is spinning, your tummy is decidedly queasy – has someone smuggled you onto a pirate ship? No, you have a hangover. You promise yourself it's the last hangover you will ever have. Oh yeah? Learn more about why you have a hangover, how you can recover from it and how you can avoid another one like it. Things will get better, promise.

Why does it hurt so much?
- You are dehydrated. Alcohol is a diuretic and removes fluids from the body – hence that awful thirst, sandpaper mouth, headache and dizziness. The alcohol has irritated your stomach and it's in a bad mood. Your partner is in a bad mood. Everybody is in a bad mood.
- You have probably only slept for a few hours. You feel tired. Your body is tired, having spent all night trying to recover from the punishment you have put it through. Everybody is tired.
- You are embarrassed about what happened, your body is

HOMEMADE REMEDIES

SORE THROAT	CUTS, BURNS AND INSECT BITES	EARACHE	NAUSEA
Gargle with some warm salted water and then drink a 50/50 mixture of fresh lemon juice and honey. You can add boiling water to the lemon and honey to make a soothing hot drink.	Undiluted lavender essential oil can be applied directly on to burns and cuts to help them heal quickly.	Apply a little warm olive oil in to the ear to relieve the pain. Keep your head at a slant when applying the oil, to avoid it slipping out over your face – you are not a salad.	Ginger is excellent for nausea – just chewing a small piece of fresh ginger can relieve the symptoms quickly.

Fully kitted up

Here are a few suggestions for your first aid kit:

- ANTISEPTIC WIPES, CREAM, LOTION (OR SPRAY)
- 2 COTTON BANDAGES AND 2 CRÊPE BANDAGES OF DIFFERENT SIZES
- A LARGE TRIANGULAR BANDAGE FOR A SLING
- ASSORTED PERFORATED SELF-ADHESIVE PLASTERS
- ASSORTED WATERPROOF PLASTERS
- 1 ROLL OF GAUZE
- A THERMOMETER
- MEASURING SPOONS
- SAFETY PINS
- SURGICAL TAPE
- SHARP SCISSORS
- TWEEZERS
- AN EYE PATCH
- EYE BATH AND EYE WASH OR PADS
- PAINKILLERS (ASPIRIN, NON-ASPIRIN AND CHILDREN'S VERSIONS)

- ANTIHISTAMINES
- ANTISEPTIC LOTION (TO HELP STOP INFECTION)
- TEA TREE OIL (A GOOD ANTISEPTIC)
- BURN OINTMENT
- CALAMINE LOTION (FOR SUNBURN)
- DECONGESTANTS (FOR STUFFY NOSE AND OTHER COLD SYMPTOMS)
- COUGH MEDICINES
- SORE THROAT SWEETS OR SPRAY
- ANTI-DIARRHOEA MEDICINE
- RE-HYDRATION SOLUTION FOR DIARRHOEA
- ANTACID MEDICINE (FOR HEARTBURN OR INDIGESTION)
- ICE PACK
- EMERGENCY CONTACT NUMBERS
- FIRST AID GUIDEBOOK

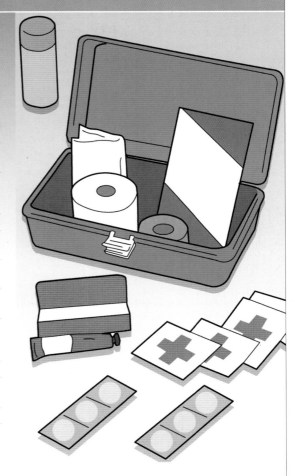

embarrassed, your friends are embarrassed. Everybody is embarrassed. Everything hurts.

What can I do about it?
- You could take a paracetamol for your headache. Aspirin may upset your stomach.
- Replace lost vitamins and minerals and flush out those toxins while rehydrating. Drink water and fruit juice. Vitamin C tablets are a good idea. A cup of ginger tea will settle your stomach. Keep drinking water.
- Try mixing together some bananas, some milk and a little honey to form a smoothie and drink it. Don't be tempted to apply the mixture to your sore head.

- Try eating some toast and if that stays down, have some eggs – they are full of cysteine, a compound that is thought to mop up the destructive chemicals that collect in the liver when it metabolizes alcohol. If you've made it to a café, order a full cooked English breakfast. If your stomach whispers 'No, can't handle that, mate' listen to it, really listen to it.
- Get more sleep if you can (in bed rather than on the bus or at your desk).
- Have a long soak in the bath and add some soothing oil. The steam will help to sweat out those nasty toxins.
- Go outside and get some fresh air, but stay out of the sun.
- Remember it won't last forever. You'll feel better the next day.

Soap

Historians assure us that soap was first made around the first century A.D. and archaeologists found what they thought to be the first soap factory in the ancient city of Pompeii. Soap, it seems, was first used for washing cloth rather than skin and was far from the gentle and pleasantly perfumed product it is today. Early versions of soap were made of fats and oils mixed with an alkaline solution. The mixture was boiled together in large vats, salt was added and when the process was complete, the soap would rise to the top of the vessel. This process was called saponification – a word worth remembering if you are ever challenged to display your extensive knowledge of personal hygiene. Don't try the vat method at home though. Just choose a scented or fragrance-free soap from the huge range available at your local supermarket. It's a much safer business.

THE SCIENCE OF SOAP

Each soap molecule is made up of carbon, hydrogen and oxygen atoms. It has a head composed of carboxyl, which is hydrophilic, i.e. loves water, and a hydrocarbon tail that is hydrophobic, i.e. afraid of water, but just adores oil and grease (does it sound like your housemate?).

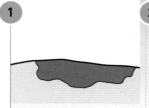  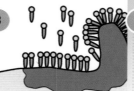 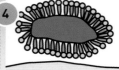

1 Your skin looks like this before a shower or bath. Attractive? Not. Time to ablute.

2 Now you're in the shower and the soap is on your skin. It has made contact and is preparing for take-off.

3 The hydrophobic end of the soap molecules, is desperate to escape. The hydrophilic end is fatally attracted to the water. It takes the grime with it as it goes.

4 Together they accomplish the mission. It's lift-off for dirt. Phew (or rather, not phew).

DOMESTIC GOD

Putting soap on the ropes

Selecting the right soap for you is a very personal affair. Don't just grab the first bar on the shelf. Ask a professional to identify your skin type and recommend a suitable soap.

Skin – scratch the surface

It helps to understand the contents of soap, but first, let's examine its target surface – your outer layer of skin or epidermis. It is thickest on your feet and thinnest on your face. You can scrub your feet with soap and water energetically but you need to be much more careful with the skin on your face.

Keep it clean, guys

Remember that if you don't wash, you will encourage germs and dirt to gather, settle and multiply on your skin. It would be like walking around covered in a filthy carpet. Not a good look. You will be covered in bugs, not hugs. Who wants to kiss a carpet covered in crumbs?

Don't slip up

Skin can be oily, dry, normal, combination or sensitive. It changes with age. If you spend time in the sun without proper protection you will damage it. Smoking, air pollution, excessive exfoliation, vigorous cleansing, too much alcohol – all of these can damage your skin. Identify and rectify.

Gently does it

Don't scrub your face too vigorously – you can strip off all the natural oils. If you have sensitive or oily skin, take extra care when choosing an appropriate soap. Vegetable glycerine soaps may suit you. If you have dry skin go for soaps with low alkaline content. Choose a gentle option with a balanced pH.

Surface tension

Next time you step into the shower, notice how water forms beads on the surface of your skin. This is because the surface tension of the water prevents it from reaching and clinging to the skin. When soap is introduced to your skin, the hydrophobic end of the soap molecule tries to get as far away from the water as possible, whereas the water-loving end is fatally attracted to the $H2O$. The result is a film that breaks the surface tension.

Fatal attraction

Your body is covered with a protective layer of oil secreted by your skin. This forms a barrier that prevents dirt and particles from entering your pores, but (sadly for some) you look dirty because the dirt trapped in the layer is visible to the naked eye. When soap is applied, the oil and grease-loving tails of the molecules attach themselves to the oily layer. When water is added, the water-loving head of the soap molecule pulls the dirty tail off the skin, removing the grime and grease with it, leaving you clean. How simple is that?

Soap opera

Today, soap is big business. Manufacturers slice it, sculpt it, square it up, scent, spice and shave it and even suspend things in it. It comes in all shapes and sizes. It stimulates, exfoliates, soothes, moisturizes, nourishes and pampers. Oh yes, and it cleans your skin, too. It's solid, sometimes slimey and slippery, squeaky clean and sensuous. It can contain essential oils, olive oil, emu oil, tea tree oil, goat's milk, honey, chocolate, grape seeds, aloe vera, the kitchen sink. Soap – you can't live without it.

Face facts

Only use deodorant soap on your body, not your face. Fragranced soap can irritate sensitive skin. Use below the neck or choose a fragrance-free alternative. Be aware that anti-bacterial soaps may kill friendly bacteria. If you want to moisturize your skin try a castile soap containing olive oil.

GARAGE

Wheels
A good bike will have aluminium-alloy wheel rims and stainless-steel spokes.

Spare Wheel
Wheels require due care and attention, and should be replaced if worn or damaged – or you'll be going nowhere.

Brakes
Without fail, check these before setting off on any journey, long or short.

'THE BEST CAR SAFETY DEVICE IS A REAR-VIEW
MIRROR WITH A COP IN IT.'
Dudley Moore

Tyres
Remember to rotate them
every couple of years to even
out tread wear.

Bodywork
Beauty isn't skin deep – a good
cleaning routine will stop your
vehicle from rusting away.

Know Your Car

Exterior

Before picking up a spanking new monkey wrench and donning a fetching set of overalls, you'll need to know a little more about what's going on outside your car. It may look pretty straightforward, but confusing your hubcap with your petrol cap will damage your car as well as your pride.

1 Windscreen: The windscreen must be scratch-free and squeaky clean. A scratch, however, does not necessarily mean a brand new windscreen. Try polishing it with glass polish or toothpaste (yes, really). Otherwise take to a windscreen repair specialist and see what they can do. Don't neglect your wipers either – they must be clean, grit-free and replaced when too worn.

2 Rear light cluster: This includes an impressive five lights: rear, brake, reversing, indicator and fog. In some countries in Europe it is a legal requirement to carry spare bulbs. Even if it's not, spares kept in the boot or glove compartment is a good idea.

3 Petrol cap: The other big decision is petrol or diesel, both of which enter the car through this device. Choosing your fuel will affect your vehicle's performance: petrol is most common and petrol-run cars are generally cheaper to buy, but diesel, with its low CO2, is fast catching on and gives more kilometres per litre (km/l) (miles per gallon (MPG))

4 Wheels and tyres: One aspect of choosing a car is deciding on front- or rear-wheel drive. In front-wheel drive cars, the entire drive chain is in the front, leaving more room for passengers and luggage. They also offer better handling in wet conditions. Basically, the front wheels pull the car along. In rear-wheel drive, the rear wheels push the car along.

5 Front light cluster: This combines the headlights, sidelights and indicator lights. They must all be working correctly at all times. Pay special attention to your indicators, which should flash between one and two times per second.

First though, a note on security. Since your car is an investment (see right) and could very well be the most expensive item you own, you don't want to lose it. One solution is choosing a car with a state-of-the-art security system. Deadlocks, for example, stop the doors from being opened even if a window has been smashed, while an electronic immobiliser will prevent the engine from working. Thieves, quite frankly, don't stand a chance.

SUIT YOURSELF

Yes, the dreaded D-word (that's 'depreciation' for anyone who's never tried reselling a car) is the bane of many a car-owner. As well as keeping your vehicle in tip-top condition for your own safety, you should also think about the future – after all, a car is a massive investment and, like any investment, you don't want to squander it.

- MAKE SURE YOUR CAR IS REGULARLY SERVICED AND CLEANED, BOTH INSIDE AND OUT. ALWAYS RETOUCH DAMAGED PAINTWORK IMMEDIATELY BEFORE IT TURNS TO RUST.

- MILEAGE ALSO COUNTS TOWARDS DEPRECIATION. DON'T EXPECT TO GET TOP WHACK FOR YOUR CAR IF YOU'VE SPENT YOUR TIME RALLYING ROUND THE GLOBE.

- BUY A CAR – AND A COLOUR – THAT IS ALREADY POPULAR, ESPECIALLY ONE THAT IS A GOOD-BUY SECOND-HAND. CERTAIN RELIABLE MAKES WILL FLY OFF THE USED-CAR LOT.

- DON'T OVERDO THE ACCESSORIES: AMAZING SPEAKERS OR FABULOUSLY PLUSH LEATHER SEATS WILL NOT ONLY LOOK OUT OF PLACE IN A £3,000-BANGER, THEY WON'T HELP RESELL IT.

- MOST CARS ARE WORTH CONSIDERABLY LESS THAN THEIR NEW COST AFTER THEIR FIRST YEAR – AND LESS THAN HALF AFTER THREE YEARS. IF PRICE BOTHERS YOU, SIMPLY BUY A USED CAR.

- DON'T SMOKE INSIDE THE CAR. OLD TOBACCO FUMES CAN LINGER LONG AFTER THE FAG'S OUT AND TURN OFF MANY WOULD-BE BUYERS.

Know Your Car

Interior

A nd now a peek inside. This is where all the action is – and as a driver this space will become your second home, or rather your second living room. If you've passed your test, you should be familiar with the various pedals and gearstick. But do you know the location of your bonnet-opening lever (crucial if you need to check the engine)? Thought not . . .

STEERING WHEEL AND HORN

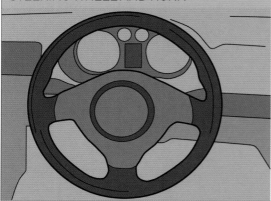

When you have both hands on the top of the wheel, there should be a slight bend in your elbows. If not, adjust the position of your seat. The indicators will be on either the left or the right of the wheel. The horn – sometimes in the centre of the wheel, sometimes on the indicator stalk – must always be working correctly. Some flashy cars may have an automatic gear-changing system attached to the wheel developed from Formula One technology, while others may include a device that enables you to change the stereo volume and settings without moving your hands from the wheel. In the event of a crash, an airbag (if fitted in your car) should stop you from hitting the wheel.

FOOT PEDALS

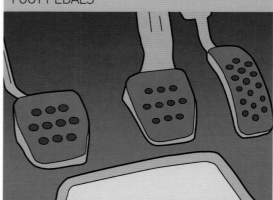

These make the car move and stop. To the right is the accelerator; this controls the speed of the car. Then there's the foot brake; touch this and your rear brake lights come on. The final pedal is the clutch, used when you move the car away, change gear and apply the brake. Some cars include cruise control: this means you can flick a switch and stop using the pedals altogether (although generally only on motorways). Automatics have no clutch pedal, but often have very large brake pedals, which can cover the equivalent space of the brake and clutch pedals on a manual. The bonnet-opening lever is often to be found in this area, but consult your car's handbook for its exact location.

A quick reminder on the importance of interior cleaning – well, you want to keep everything in full working order and your car from depreciating, don't you? Seats should be vacuumed regularly, floors swept and the dashboard and armrests wiped with a cleanser and damp chamois leather (we did warn you it was like a living room).

GEARSTICK

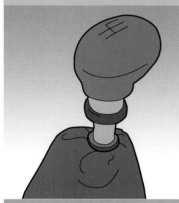

Whether your car is an automatic or a manual, you'll still have a gearstick. This controls the gears, which in turn control the speed of the car in relation to the terrain and weather. However, the position of the stick can vary. Some older cars, for instance, have the gearstick mounted on the steering column (in essentially the same position as a huge indicator), while others have it situated on the dashboard.

HANDBRAKE

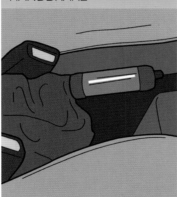

Necessary for emergency stops and to prevent your parked vehicle from sliding down a hill. A properly adjusted handbrake should click four to five times from being fully off before reaching the 'on' position. And again, there can be variations on the handbrake position. Some cars, for instance, have a handbrake situated in the footwell near to the driving pedals, creating a footbrake that serves the same purpose as a handbrake. Confusing stuff!

SEAT MECHANISM

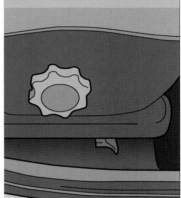

Necessary for adjusting the seat. Cars generally have one lever to alter the forward/backward position, and another to alter the reclining position. Some cars also have levers to adjust the height. A very posh car could include a computer-controlled seating system, which cleverly recognises your preferred position and changes it accordingly. Note that an incorrectly positioned seat – in other words, one where you can't easily reach the foot pedals – could result in loss of control.

Basic Car Kit

A few bags of shopping, a pair of old wellies and an old cagoule in your boot will be no use whatsoever if you break down. What you really need to be carrying, boring as it may seem, is a tool kit. And no, the spare tyre and jack supplied with your car aren't sufficient. The following items – plus some know-how – will help release your inner grease monkey to fix most minor car troubles. Something not quite right with your car can have a huge impact on its performance, and the long arm of the law can come down on you pretty heavily for any infringements. Make the investment and be prepared – you'll be glad you did.

PRESSURE GAUGE

Ideally, keep this in your glove compartment – gauges in garages aren't that accurate.

PLIERS

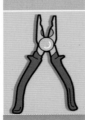

The tweezers of the tool world have a million and one uses.

SCREWDRIVERS

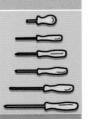

Make sure to have a set that includes a flathead and a Phillips.

SPANNERS

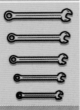

Buy a Russian Doll set, covering a range from 10–19mm.

WHEEL BRACE

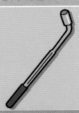

Best to get one that has an extending handle – essential for removing nuts!

CLEAN CLOTH

It gets dirty so that you don't have to.

FOR THE SUPER-CAUTIOUS

Striking a balance between taking up too much space and having the necessary equipment to get you out of trouble is a tricky thing. If you're of a nervous disposition then the following will also come in handy.

INSULATING TAPE

May well come in handy if there is a loose electrical connection.

FIRE EXTINGUISHER

Keep this handy under one of the seats, as when it comes to tackling a fire speed is the essence.

WARNING TRIANGLE

Obligatory if travelling in mainland Europe. Put it at least 50m (152ft) behind your car.

SPARE BULBS

This is regarded as compulsory on the Continent, and, at any rate, a good idea.

Windscreen de-icer spray and scraper
If it's icy you'll be glad that you remembered this double act.

Spare fuses (10, 20 and 30 amp)
For when an electrical circuit breaks.

Can of WD40
Helpful when there's a wet, muggy atmosphere outside. Conditions such as fog can make the engine go damp; a quick spritz of this will kick-start it back into action.

Engine oil
Make sure it's the right grade for your engine.

Windscreen washer fluid with additive

Empty petrol container

Spare fan belt/ drivebelt
Failing that, a pair of tights borrowed from a female acquaintance.

Tow rope/chain

Travel rugs

Touch-up paint
To instantly go over any stone chippings before the damage gets rusty.

FIRST AID KIT

Always carry a first aid kit and remember that it is compulsory in parts of mainland Europe.

MOBILE PHONE

Perfect for summoning help (as well as checking the footie scores). Don't use when driving though.

CAR HANDBOOK

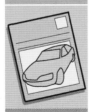

You'd be surprised at the number of people who leave this at home. Where it's of no use whatsoever.

TORCH

If there's a problem with your car, odds on it'll be dark and you'll have to peer under the bonnet.

Funnel

Tool Box Essentials

A surgeon without his instruments is useless. Likewise, a mechanic – however amateur – needs the correct kit. Before getting dirty, invest in the tools illustrated on the facing page since the ones supplied with your car will not be sufficient. Pack as much as you can in your boot – breakdowns have a nasty habit of being utterly unexpected – and store the remainder in your garage for the basic home maintenance you're about to learn.

LOOKING AFTER THE MOTOR

Remember to keep your car in good nick. That means cleaning the windows and body regularly (more about this on pages 158 and 159). You should also touch up any scratches as soon as they appear – it'll save you a bigger job later on.

Clean cloths: Have a few to hand so you don't get too grubby. Use old newspaper to mop up any big spills.

Windscreen washer fluid: Your washers must always have enough fluid, or you'll be left high and dry.

Cleansers and waxes: Gear necessary for cleaning and servicing.

Touch-up paint: Keep this handy to immediately paint over a scratch before any rust sets in.

Before you start tinkering, bear in mind the following Rules for Tools:

Rule one: invest in the best

As with most things in life, you get what you pay for. When choosing your tools, buy the best you can afford. Cheap tools have a short lifespan and could even damage your vehicle. If you buy a top-quality kit, it really will last you a lifetime. If you're restricted to a tight budget, however, spend top whack on the tools that you're likely to use the most, namely a good set of screwdrivers, some pliers and an adjustable spanner.

Rule two: treat tools with TLC

No, TLC isn't OTT. Don't leave your tools hanging around; instead keep them stored neatly together in a tool box. Ensure they are always clean and never, ever leave them wet – they'll only get rusty. And therefore useless. If you leave your tools unused for any length of time, cover the metal parts with a thin layer of oil or grease. This will ensure that they will stay as fresh as the day you bought them.

Rule three: be gentle, please

Your car may be pretty hardcore but it's hardly a tank, so learn to use your tools correctly or you could end up damaging your motor for good. Spanners, for instance, should always be turned towards you as this gives you more control. Another tip is to never over-tighten nuts and bolts. If you're unsure of your own strength, buy a torque wrench, a smart tool that makes a loud clicking sound when the correct amount of force has been applied.

A light touch is again necessary for any hammer work. Small dents, for example, can be lightly tapped out using a hammer covered in a cloth. But if you think you may be too heavy-handed, leave this job to the professionals.

Screwdrivers should be used for just that purpose – driving in screws – and not as general-purpose levers or chisels. This will only wreck the head of the screwdriver and bend the body out of shape.

Rule four: don't be dirty

Car maintenance can get messy. Whether you're under the bonnet or changing a tyre, wear clothes you don't mind ruining (overalls are best). Have heaps of clean rags and sheets of newspaper handy, remove any jewellery and protect your hands with plastic gloves – surgical gloves, available from most chemists, are ideal. You're now ready to go. Good luck!

BOX OF DELIGHTS

Amateur mechanics should make sure they have access to all the tools below and store them all together in a sturdy tool box in the garage.

1. Jack: Lifts the car up so you can then change the wheel.

2. Torque wrench: This will make a loud click when the exact amount of force required for the nut and bolt has been applied. Very clever.

3. Wheel brace: Vital if you need to get a wheel off.

4. Screwdrivers: At least one of each type is necessary.

5. Spanners: Having a 10–19mm set in your tool box should cover your needs.

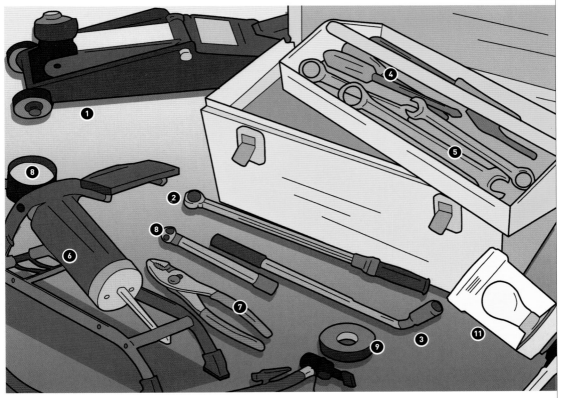

6. Tyre pump: To inflate your tyres (including your spare) when they get too low.

7. Pliers: Always useful for tightening and undoing various components.

8. Tyre pressure gauge: Vital for checking that your tyre pressures, including your spare, are correct – look in your car handbook for the exact measurements

9. Insulating tape: Crucial for patching up any electrical circuits that may need repairing.

10. Spare bulbs and fuses: (Not shown.) You never know when your bulbs might pop. 10-, 20- and 30-amp fuses will sort a broken circuit.

11. Torch: Perfect for those hard-to-see problem areas.

Basic Maintenance and Repairs

F irst, a few safety measures. Remove any watches and rings and put on some overalls and a pair of plastic gloves – you'll not only look the part, you'll also keep things clean and safe from the off. Keep the garage door open for ventilation and don't smoke – you don't want your car turning into a mini bomb. Read the manual before tinkering – it contains all the information you'll need to know and never work on a blazing hot engine. The following Chore Chart is based on the assumption that you drive daily. Follow the instructions religiously and not only will you save money on repair bills, you will also reduce some of the depreciation that is inevitable when it comes to reselling the car.

CHORE CHART: WHAT TO DO WHEN

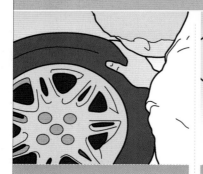
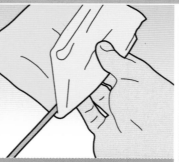
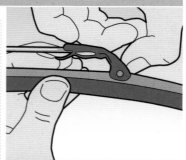

DAILY:
- INSPECT FOR FLAT TYRES
- WALK AROUND THE CAR AND ENSURE NOTHING IS DAMAGED, PAYING SPECIAL ATTENTION TO BOTH FRONT AND REAR LIGHTS
- CHECK THE LIGHTS AND INDICATORS ARE WORKING CORRECTLY
- MAKE SURE WINDSCREENS AND WINDOWS ARE CLEAN
- TEST THE BRAKES WORK BY SQUEEZING THE PEDAL SHORTLY AFTER DRIVING OFF

WEEKLY:
- CHECK THE FUEL LEVEL – THIS SHOULD ALWAYS BE ABOVE THE HALFWAY MARK – AND LOOK FOR ANY LEAKS
- INSPECT THE OIL; AGAIN, THIS SHOULD BE ABOVE THE HALFWAY MARK ON THE DIPSTICK. ALSO LOOK FOR LEAKS
- CHECK THE BRAKE AND CLUTCH FLUID AND LOOK FOR LEAKS
- EXAMINE THE COOLANT LEVEL IN THE RADIATOR – THIS SHOULD BE DONE WHEN THE ENGINE IS COLD. AND AGAIN, LOOK FOR LEAKS
- MAKE SURE THERE'S SUFFICIENT FLUID IN THE WINDSCREEN WASHER RESERVOIR
- ASK SOMEONE TO HELP YOU CHECK THE BRAKE LIGHTS
- CHECK THE BATTERY CONNECTIONS ARE TIGHT AND CLEAN AND TOP UP WITH DISTILLED WATER – NEVER TAP – IF NECESSARY (YOU WON'T HAVE TO DO THIS IF THE BATTERY IS SEALED)

MONTHLY:
- TEST YOUR TYRES' PRESSURE WHEN THEY ARE COLD – AND DON'T FORGET THE SPARE. ALSO CHECK THE TYRE TREAD
- MAKE SURE THE FAN BELT IS SUFFICIENTLY TIGHT AND IS NOT WORN
- CHECK THE WIPER BLADES. REPLACE IF WORN
- GIVE THE CAR A THOROUGH CLEAN AND POLISH
- IF YOU NORMALLY ONLY USE THE CAR FOR SHORT TRIPS, TAKE IT OUT ON A LONGER RUN. THIS IS GOOD FOR THE ENGINE AND RECHARGES THE BATTERY

EVERY SIX MONTHS OR SO:
- CHECK COMPONENTS – AIR FILTER, FUEL FILTER AND SPARK PLUGS SHOULD BE CHANGED AT THE SERVICE INTERVALS RECOMMENDED IN YOUR HANDBOOK. THIS SHOULD BE CARRIED OUT WHEN YOU TAKE YOUR CAR IN FOR ITS SERVICE.

X NO-NOS

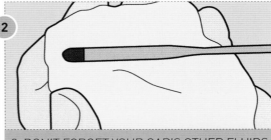

1. DON'T LEAVE THE FUEL TANK LESS THAN HALF FULL

This might sound overly cautious, but you should always leave the tank at least half full. If it starts running dry, the sediment from the tank could end up in the fuel system. This in turn could cause the engine to stall and lead to more serious problems. A half-empty tank will also attract water vapour. And another fuel point: don't keep changing the grade as this will only confuse your engine. Stick to what the handbook recommends.

2. DON'T FORGET YOUR CAR'S OTHER FLUIDS

This means the oil, brake fluid, clutch fluid and coolant. You should check their levels weekly and also inspect for any leaks. If you neglect the oil, for instance, you could end up damaging your engine and spending a fortune on repairs. Similarly, getting amnesia over the coolant in your radiator could result in your engine overheating. A five-minute check should mean stress-free driving.

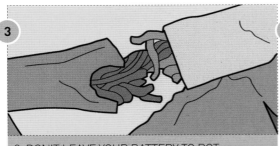

3. DON'T LEAVE YOUR BATTERY TO ROT

Any repairs to your car's electrical system should really be left to the professionals. But this doesn't mean you can forget it altogether as a faulty battery is a prime cause of breakdowns. First switch off the engine. Then check the outside of the battery for any damage and make sure the cables aren't fraying. Most batteries are maintenance-free. Some, however, require regular inspection of the electrolyte level – you may need to top this up with distilled water. If a white, powdery deposit has formed on the terminals, pour hot water over them and then coat with Vaseline.

4. DON'T OVERLOOK YOUR TYRES

These are your only contact with the road, so treat them with the respect they deserve. Good tread is necessary for difficult weather conditions and road surfaces; if the tread reaches 1.6mm (1/15in) it's too worn and the tyre should be replaced immediately. As for the pressure, look in your car handbook to find out the correct level for your vehicle and the type of tyres fitted. Under-inflated tyres damage more quickly. They also increase your vehicle's overall fuel consumption. Over-inflated tyres wear more rapidly. Costly either way.

Under Pressure

A lways buy the right tyres for your make of car and for your driving conditions – and always aim for the best ones you can afford. For tyre maintenance, you'll need two distinct tools: a tread gauge and a tyre pressure gauge. It's worth investing in your own since pressure gauges at petrol stations can be wildly inaccurate. In theory you can use a coin to inspect the tread, but that, too, is likely to be way off the mark.

CHECKING YOUR TYRE PRESSURE

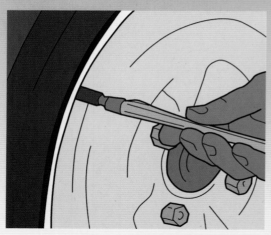

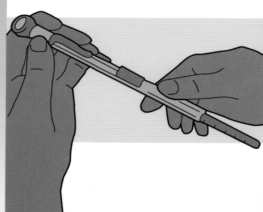

Having the correct pressure is of the utmost importance – both under- and over-inflated tyres wear much more quickly. Tyre pressure can decrease as the temperature drops, so check regularly, especially during the winter months.

1. Check the pressure when the tyres are cold (this means they haven't been driven for at least 30 minutes). If they're still warm, you could get a misleading reading.

2. The pressure is measured in metric bars or pounds per square inch (psi). The correct pressure for your car can be found in its manual. The front and rear tyres often have different settings.

3. Remove the cap from the valve stem.

4. Press the rounded end of the gauge against the valve stem. Make sure no air escapes.

5. Remove the gauge.

6. Read the measurement using the ruler end of the gauge.

7. Repeat with all four tyres.

8. Oh, and don't forget the spare!

CHECKING YOUR TYRE TREAD

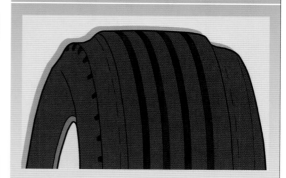

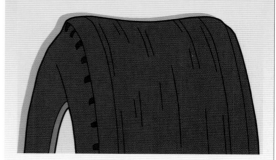

IN THE BALANCE

Even the most box-fresh of tyres will have some irregularities. The solution? Get your tyres balanced regularly to stop any wobbling. This is another job for the mechanic – don't ever attempt this at home.

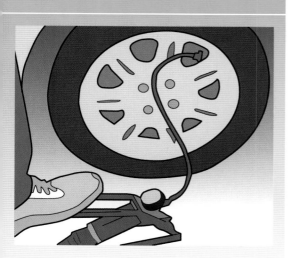

If the tyre pressure is too high:
Gently press the pin in the centre of the tyre valve to release air. Do a little at a time.

And if it is too low:
Visit your nearest petrol station as soon as possible for more air from the compressed air machine, or if you have your own pump, use that.

Good tread is necessary for difficult weather conditions and road surfaces; if the tread reaches 1.6mm (1/15in) it's too worn and the tyre should be replaced immediately. You should check each tyre at two different points. While checking your tyre tread, also look for signs of wear.

Another top tip is rotating your tyres to even out tread wear – in other words, replacing the two front ones with the rear ones periodically. Ask a mechanic to do this and include the spare tyre in the rotation, unless it's a compact spare.

If the tread is worn out more on one side, this could mean that the tyres need to be aligned. A visit to a mechanic or tyre specialist should sort this out.

Liquid News

Your car needs a surprising amount of juice to keep it running smoothly – namely oil, coolant, brake fluid, hydraulic clutch fluid and maybe even power steering fluid. All these fluids need their levels checking regularly, and all need to be inspected for leaks.

OIL

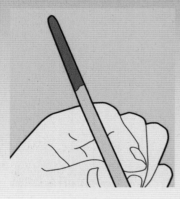 

If your engine doesn't have the correct amount of oil – in the right grade – it could end up seriously damaged. Check with your car handbook for the type of oil that's right for your car. To check your oil . . .

1. Make sure the engine is cold and that the car is on a level surface.

2. The instrument used to check the oil is called the dipstick. Pull it out and wipe it with a clean cloth. Return it fully, pull out again and check the oil mark.

3. Try not to let the oil level slip below halfway; likewise, it shouldn't be over-full.

To fill up:

1. Find the oil filler cap (it's usually marked 'oil').

2. Unscrew it and pour in a small quantity of oil – a funnel may help.

3. Wait a few seconds and then recheck the level with the dipstick.

4. Wipe off any oil you may have spilled.

5. Refit the filler cap – make sure it's tight – and ensure that the dipstick is pushed fully back into its tube.

6. A final tip: never over-fill the engine with oil as this could cause leaks. This is why you should fill it little by little.

COOLANT

Coolant is a mixture of one-third anti-freeze and two-thirds water. It stops your engine from getting too hot (and from freezing) and also prevents rusting inside your radiator. Check your handbook to make sure you use the right one.

1. Park your car on level ground. Open the bonnet and look for a plastic container marked with 'Min' and 'Max' levels.

2. Check the level when the engine is cold. The level should be near the maximum point. If not, unscrew the cap and top it up with coolant.

3. Also check for leaks. If you have to fill up the container often (say, every two months), there might be a leak. Seek professional help.

POWER STEERING FLUID

Your car may also need power steering fluid, so check in the handbook whether there's a separate reservoir for this too. If so, top up with the appropriate fluid recommended by your manufacturer, using the same directions as suggested below under 'clutch fluid'.

DOMESTIC GOD

Any fluid check can get messy, so wear a pair of plastic gloves and have a clean rag handy. Brake fluid is particularly nasty – it has many of the same properties as paint stripper, so wash any spillages off your skin as soon as there's contact.

BRAKE FLUID

If the brake fluid gets too low your brakes will work inefficiently – or not at all. Checking your brakes must be done as swiftly as possible because brakes don't like contact with air or any moisture.

1. Make sure the car is parked on level ground. Open the bonnet and locate the brake fluid reservoir – it should be located behind your engine.

2. Unscrew the cap and check the level. If it is below the 'Max' mark, top up. Always use fluid from a new container – exposure to air, however fleeting, contaminates it, so dispose of any remainder.

3. Also check the quality of the fluid by dipping a finger in and then rubbing the liquid between your hands. If it feels gritty, get a mechanic to change it.

4. As the brakes wear, the fluid level will drop – this is normal. But if you're topping up the levels on a regular basis, there may be a leak. Get this fixed immediately.

CLUTCH FLUID

For this, somewhat confusingly, you also use brake fluid – check with your car handbook for the correct grade. The clutch sometimes shares a common reservoir with the brake fluid; look in your car handbook for details. The clutch fluid ensures the smooth operation of the clutch when you change gears. If your vehicle has a mechanical clutch – as opposed to hydraulic – there will be no clutch fluid reservoir.

1. Park on level ground. Open your bonnet – the clutch fluid reservoir should be behind the engine.

2. The level should be between 'Min' and 'Max'.

3. If you need to top up, unscrew the cap and top up with new fluid – always use a freshly opened bottle. Again, dispose of the leftovers.

4. If there is a massive loss, there could be a leak. Seek professional advice immediately.

I Can See Clearly Now

Windscreens, believe it or not, are easy to overlook when it comes to car maintenance. The reckoning being that since the driver is staring out of it daily, any problems will be obvious. Wrong. Bet you haven't considered your wipers (blades that work properly are actually a legal requirement). Or, indeed, your washer reservoir . . .

BRAKE FLUID

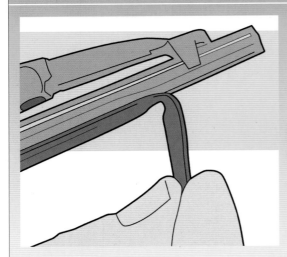

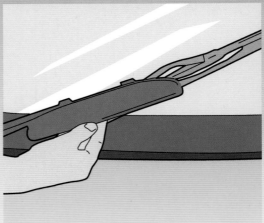

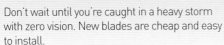

Don't wait until you're caught in a heavy storm with zero vision. New blades are cheap and easy to install.

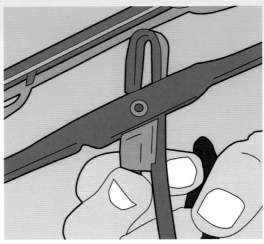

1. Every now and then, check the blades for baldness – and don't forget your rear wiper blade. You need to make sure all blades are working efficiently.

2. Lift the arm from the screen, check the blade rubber and then wipe the edge of the blade with some windscreen washer fluid and a cloth.

3. Do the blades squeak? Do they smear? If so, you'll need to replace them with new ones. Make sure you buy the right blades for the make and model of your car.

DOMESTIC GOD

Consider carrying some windscreen washer fluid in your boot – you never know when you'll need it. And another tip: don't use a higher wiper speed than necessary when it's raining, as this will only make your blades wear down more quickly.

WASHER RESERVOIR MAINTENANCE

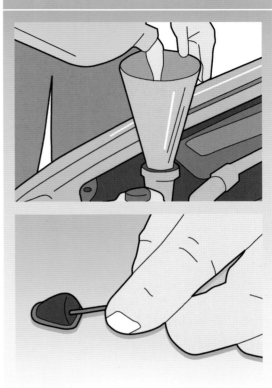

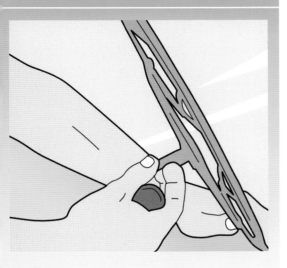

4. To fit new blades: first, turn the ignition off.

5. Lift up the wiper arm until it locks.

6. Remove the blade. Turn it at right angles to the wiper arm, then slide it out. Don't let the arm ping back.

7. Fit the new blade – check the packet for precise details – and then lower the arm back into position on the windscreen.

8. Check the wipers are working correctly before driving off.

9. During winter your blades may stick to the windscreen. You can free them using de-icer.

You should check this weekly as well.

1. Open the bonnet – yes, confusingly, the reservoir is under here. The rear wiper generally uses the same reservoir; if not, it will be in the boot.

2. The reservoir should be full. If it's not, fill up with washer fluid using a funnel. You can even buy specially formulated fluids for summer (fluid that can remove dead insects) and winter (fluid that won't freeze). If you do choose seasonal fluids, though, remember to swap them over when the seasons change.

3. Also check the nozzles. These spray the fluid onto the windscreen and can easily get clogged up. Clean away any gunk using something pointy like a needle and work it down the eye of the jet. At the same time make sure they are properly positioned. Reposition with your fingers.

Shampooing Your Car

Beauty isn't skin deep. When it comes to cars, a good cleanse, tone and moisturise routine will not only stop your vehicle from rusting away, it will also make it easier to resell. Keep your car buffed and beautiful and everything should be just peachy. After all, don't you want to look good on the road?

CLEANING KIT

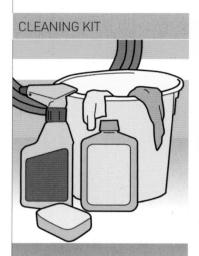

- CAR SHAMPOO
- SPONGE
- BUCKET
- HOSE
- PLENTY OF CLEAN CLOTHS
- BRUSH FOR THE TYRES
- WAX
- CHROME/METAL POLISH
- CHAMOIS LEATHER
- VACUUM CLEANER WITH SLIM HEAD
- VARIOUS CLEANERS FOR THE INTERIOR

WASHING AND WAXING

1. Wait until the car is cold. And don't clean your car in direct sunlight – the same goes for drying.

2. Start with the wheels. Spray the tyres; then clean with a brush and plenty of car shampoo and water.

3. Now concentrate on the body. Start at the roof and work down, cleaning with lots of shampoo and a sponge. Rinse thoroughly using the hose, all the while looking for any scratches or chips. Dry with a chamois leather.

CLEANING THE ENGINE

Use a clean cloth to wipe away any dirt and grease from the reservoirs, the radiator, under the bonnet and the battery. This will not only make the engine look good, but it will also help to keep it running smoothly.

DOMESTIC GOD

Don't forget your windows . . .
Treat them like the windows of your house. Spritz with a glass cleaner (use one that's been specially formulated for a car), then wipe with a chamois leather. And don't forget your windscreen – it's not fair to leave your wipers with all the work. And don't smoke inside the car – this only makes the windows even dirtier.

DEALING WITH RUST, SCRATCHES AND DENTS

Any rust should be tackled the moment it's discovered. Scrape it with a wire brush and follow this with emery paper. Then use a special rust treatment, available from all good car shops. Finish with a dab of touch-up paint, which comes either in brush or aerosol form – make sure you get the exact shade.

If you find a scratch, clean round it with water, then paint over using the touch-up paint. Do this slowly and carefully in the same direction. Wait for a few days for everything to settle, then rub the area with a polishing compound to blend the new paint in.

A small dent can be lightly tapped out using a hammer covered in a cloth. But, as with all of the above, if you don't feel fully confident doing the job, leave it to the professionals. You could end up doing further damage to your car.

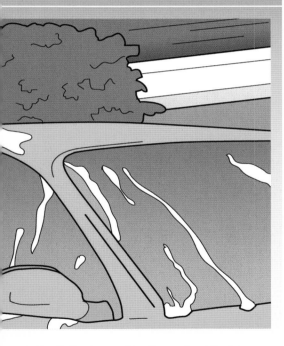

CLEANING THE INTERIOR

4. Now it's time to wax – this will prevent rust. Don't do this in strong sunlight, either. Liquid waxes are easiest to use.

5. Put the wax on with one cloth, wipe off and buff with another. Work in one small area at a time.

6. Finally, polish the chrome and metal bits (such as handles) with a specially formulated polish.

We've already compared the inside of your car to your living room – so treat it accordingly. Start with decluttering – remove any empty drink cans and sweet wrappers. Then vacuum the seats, paying special attention to the backs of the seats where crumbs like to gather. Remove any spills with a suitable stain remover. Move to the floor, remembering to remove the rubber mats. End with the details – the dashboard and armrests – using a cleanser compatible with the material. A wipe with the damp chamois may be sufficient here.

Troubleshooting Q&A

I f your car won't start, it could be something as simple as there being no fuel in the tank. On the other hand, it could be something more serious. Use a methodical approach to diagnose the possible cause. If it's easy to solve, then fix it using this book. If not, then seek professional help immediately. Driving with a fault is simply not worth the risk.

PROBLEM

CAR WON'T START ▶

Hmmm, you've turned the key but can't get your car to start.

ODD SOUND WHEN STARTING UP ▶

When you start up the car, there's a funny whirring sound.

BATTERY LIGHT COMES ON ▶

The battery light on the dashboard is glowing red while you are driving – it feels like a warning.

SPONGY BRAKES ▶

When you push the brake pedal it feels spongy. And not very safe.

HISSING NOISE ▶

When you stop the car, you can hear a hissing sound from under the bonnet.

CAUSE & SOLUTION

FUEL LEVEL OR BATTERY ▶

Is the fuel tank empty? Is the battery flat? If you're still having no joy, then there could be an electrical problem, so visit a mechanic.

STARTER MOTOR OR DRIVESHAFT ▶

This could be down to a defective starter motor or a dodgy driveshaft. Both require professional assistance.

BATTERY ▶

It is: your battery could be flat or your engine may not be working. Turn off the ignition, inspect the battery, then seek professional help.

BRAKE FLUID ▶

Check the brake fluid – is it at the right level? Otherwise you could be experiencing trouble with your callipers or hoses, another job for a mechanic.

RADIATOR ▶

Open the bonnet – cautiously – and look at the radiator. Is there an obvious leak or fault? If not, it's off to the mechanic again.

PROBLEM

GEARS FEEL CLUNKY ▶

There's a clunky sound – and feeling – when you're changing gears.

SQUEAKY BRAKES ▶

You squeeze the brake pedal to stop – and it squeaks.

LIQUID UNDER CAR ▶

There's a puddle of liquid on the road under your car.

CAR STALLS ▶

Your car stalls more often than it should in cold weather.

STEERING FEELS UNSAFE ▶

You're suddenly finding it very difficult to steer.

CAUSE & SOLUTION

GEARBOX ▶

Check the transmission fluid level. If the problem persists, you may need assistance. Don't leave this fault too long as it could get expensive.

BRAKE PADS ▶

Is this a new thing? Some brakes simply squeak. But if yours are usually as silent as a (non-squeaky) mouse, you may need new pads.

FLUIDS ▶

First identify the liquid. If it's water, don't worry – it's simply a by-product of your air conditioning. Anything else (oil, coolant or other fluid) means a leak, so consult a mechanic.

BATTERY OR AIR FILTER ▶

Check the air filter and the battery – both can cause your car to stall. Still no luck? Then call a mechanic.

TYRES OR WHEELS ▶

Your tyres should be the first place you look – check for flats and low pressure. Otherwise it could be your wheels, which will require professional assistance.

Ready, Steady . . . Go!
The Ten-minute Road Check

O n the road, you may feel less vulnerable than a motorcycle and less precarious than a bike, but that doesn't mean you're invincible. If you're thoughtless with your maintenance, you could harm yourself as well as others. So be good and do a quick run-through of the following pointers as often as possible – in an ideal world, this would be every time you set out or at the start of any long journey.

1 **Mirrors:** Check all mirrors are correctly positioned and look for any cracks.

2 **Lights:** The headlights and rear lights, sidelights, brake lights, fog lights and indicators must all be working properly. Replace any dead bulbs immediately.

3 **Fuel:** The tank should be always at least half full. After all that hard work, you don't want to be caught short!

4 **Wheels and tyres:** It's wise to do a visual check before every journey. Keep a lookout for any cuts and debris, and monitor the general wear and state of the tread. Make sure the tyres are inflated to the correct pressure. And don't forget the spare.

5 **Windscreen:** A good windscreen is one without any cracks, scratches or smears. Make sure the wiper blades aren't worn, and that the washer reservoir is filled up to the top.

6 **Fluids:** Check the following and, if necessary, top up: the engine oil, the brake fluid, the coolant, the hydraulic clutch fluid and, where necessary, the power steering fluid. Also look for any leaks.

7 **Fan belt:** This must be tensioned correctly and damage-free.

8 **Horn:** This must be hooting properly.

9 **Brakes:** Drive off for a short distance and then test your brakes – they shouldn't feel spongy. If there are any problems, stop driving, check the brake fluid level or call a mechanic immediately. Don't forget the handbrake – this must also work perfectly at all times.

Know Your Bike

Understanding Your Wheels

So you've deliberated, cogitated and are now the proud owner of the perfect bike. But there's still more to learn. Once bikes were made from steel and plastics – pretty basic stuff. Now it's NASA all the way, with lightweight materials such as carbon fibre and titanium used on aerodynamic bikes created by high-tech computer design.

1 Handlebars: All you really need to know is that you have three options: drop (found on racers and some touring bikes), flat (found on roadsters, hybrids and utility bikes) and riser (again, a feature of utility as well as mountain bikes). What suits you is all down to personal preference.

2 Saddle: Comfort is key. Saddles are available in a wide range of materials, shapes, sizes and padding. The only way to know what's right for you is to sit on as many as possible. Do consider gel-filled saddles, though, as the gel moulds round the rider's bum. Hey presto, a bespoke seat!

3 Braking system: Cantilever and V-brakes squeeze the wheel rim (the part of the wheel closest to the tyre) to stop the bike. Hub-mounted brakes work in a similar way but at the hub (the centre of the wheel). Hydraulic brakes operate in a similar way to those on a car.

4 Gearing system: Derailleur gears (pictured) are most common – as the gears change, the chain 'derails' from one sprocket to another. You can also get hub gears. These have a gearbox built into the hub (centre) of the rear wheel.

5 Wheels: Consist of the tyre, tube, rim, spokes and hub. A good bike will have aluminium alloy wheel rims (the part of the wheel that touches the tyre), which are light and rust-free. Also look out for stainless steel spokes, as they're less likely to corrode.

And it doesn't stop there. Front and rear suspension is another advancement – this is now standard on many mountain bikes, allowing riders to navigate pretty much any sort of terrain. And then there are the gears: originally, three were the norm; now some bikes can have 27 or more. Exhausting, no? Don't fret, though: the basic stuff to do with how the bike works – the pedalling, steering and braking – has remained the same since the days of the penny-farthing.

TOP TIPS

There's a huge range of bicycles and bicycle retailers out there. Before you buy, cast an eye over this list to help you get the most from your new set of wheels:

What kind of bike?
First of all, decide on the kind of cycling you'll want to be doing – nipping round town or churning up mud at weekends? Which is more important – comfort, smoothness or speed?

Buy from a reputable bike shop
This may be more costly, but better to get your bike from someone you trust and can talk to properly, whether your a first-timer or a seasoned pro, rather than a dealer out to make a fast buck. They also won't mind you asking what may to you seem stupid questions.

Budget
Spend to the max: more expense = better quality = a better ride = greater pleasure. And allow space in your budget for at least the bare minimum essentials: lock, helmet and lights.

Sizing
Ensure a comfortable ride by standing over the middle of the toptube (running from the handlebar stem to the saddle) with your feet about 12 inches apart. You should be able to lift the front wheel one or two inches.

Test ride
Any dealer worth their salt will let you take your prospective purchase out for a quick spin before you buy.

Know your stuff
Do as much research as possible before setting foot in the shop. You'll be less likely to have the wool pulled over your eyes.

Basic Bike Kit

Put those cowboy boots away. What you'll need, boring as it may sound, are sensible shoes, tight-fitting-yet-flexible clothes, and a helmet. If necessary and you want to arrive somewhere smart, carry a change of clothes in your backpack. Your bike could do with accessorising, too, otherwise it might feel left out. Here are some suggestions for equipment and clothing suitable for all kinds of weather.

SHIRT	CYCLING SHORTS	SHOES	FLEECE	CYCLING GLOVES	RAINY WEATHER GEAR

Day-glo colours, especially yellow, will get you noticed.	Not just a fashion relic from the 1980s. These will keep you cool and comfortable in warm weather.	You can buy cycling shoes designed for compatibility with pedals, but trainers are fine.	The best way to stay warm. Different levels of thickness mean different levels of insulation.	Usually fingerless with mesh backs and gel-filled palms. Great for comfort on long rides.	The best gear is made from fabric that stops water getting in while allowing perspiration out.

HELMET HELP

The vast majority of fatal bike accidents are caused by an injury to the head. Wearing a helmet is still not a legal must – but you'd be a fool to go without. In fact, nowadays, you're more likely to get funny looks if you're NOT wearing one. Here are some tips about what to look for:

1. Choose a dealer with a wide selection. Helmets must reach certain safety standards. In the UK, the safest ones are those that have passed the Snell Foundation test.

2. A good-quality helmet should offer plenty of ventilation, with lots of air channels running from front to back.

3. The helmet should sit low on your brow, but high enough to allow clear vision upwards and sideways. A two-finger gap between eyebrows and helmet should be sufficient.

4. Is the fit correct? When the chinstrap is properly adjusted and fastened, you should not be able to move the helmet backwards and forwards with your hands.

5. Also consider a nape strap. If properly fitted (fractionally below the bulge in the skull), it should stop the helmet from slipping back.

6. Replace the helmet after every crash, however minor, and again after every two or three years. The inside foam won't stay supple forever.

LIGHTS

Cyclists are legally required to ride with a white light at the front and a red at the rear.

PANNIER

This is a holdall that fits onto a cycle rack, usually at the back of the bike. Good for heavy loads.

LOCK

A heavy-duty D-lock will provide the best security for your bike. You may want to invest in a second lock if you're cycling in the urban jungle.

MUDGUARDS

Crucial in winter, unless you actually like the muddy look.

REFLECTORS

Essential for night riding and a necessary backup for lights.

WATER BOTTLE

Because cycling can be thirsty work, especially in hot weather.

PUMP

Ensure this fits your tyre valve type.

MULTI-TOOL

This very clever device contains spanners and Allen keys of several different sizes.

Bike Maintenance and Repairs

T he bicycle is officially the world's favourite vehicle: an estimated eight out of ten people worldwide own, or have access to, a bike. But do you think all these people have the first clue about what to do when they get a puncture? Or a loose chain? Of course not, but with a little application and learning, you can be one of the practical few. Bike repairs in general are not too tricky; they just require a little know-how and some common sense. The same goes for general maintenance. If you give your cycle the right amount of TLC, it will last you for the rest of your life. How's that for an investment?

CHORE CHART: WHAT TO DO WHEN

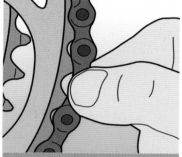
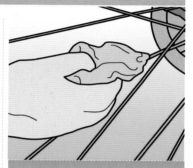

DAILY:
- CHECK THE BRAKES. RIDE A FEW METRES THEN GIVE THEM A GOOD SQUEEZE – YOU SHOULD ONLY HAVE TO PULL HALFWAY DOWN FOR THEM TO PROPERLY WORK. IF THEY'RE NOT WORKING, DON'T USE THE BIKE.
- TYRES. CHECK PRESSURE AND GIVE THEM THE ONCE-OVER FOR STRAY DEBRIS (SUCH AS NAILS).
- WHEELS. MAKE SURE THE SPOKES AREN'T DAMAGED AND THAT THE WHEELS ARE 'TRUE' AND CORRECTLY ALIGNED.
- TEST THE LIGHTS.
- CHECK THE BELL.
- CHECK THE SADDLE IS TIGHT – THERE SHOULD BE NO MOVEMENT.
- GIVE THE BIKE A QUICK ALL-OVER WIPE WITH A CLOTH.

FORTNIGHTLY:
- MAKE SURE THE CHAIN IS OILED AND PROPERLY ADJUSTED.
- LOOK AT THE BRAKE PADS (THE PART OF THE BRAKE THAT TOUCHES THE WHEEL RIM WHEN THE BRAKE LEVER IS APPLIED). THERE SHOULD BE LOTS OF RUBBER LEFT AND AT LEAST 1MM (1/16IN) BETWEEN THE PAD AND THE RIM OF THE WHEEL.
- CHECK THE HEADSET FOR SMOOTH STEERING MOVEMENT, PAYING PARTICULAR ATTENTION TO ANY MOVEMENT BETWEEN THE FORKS (THE TUBE THAT ATTACHES YOUR HANDLEBARS TO YOUR WHEELS) AND THE FRAME. ANY PROBLEMS AND YOUR BIKE COULD BE DIFFICULT TO CONTROL.
- HOLD ONE PEDAL STILL AND TRY TO MOVE THE OTHER. IF THERE'S ANY MOVEMENT, YOU SHOULD TIGHTEN THE BOLTS.

MONTHLY:
- CHECK THE LUBRICATION ON THE BRAKES, HUBS, GEARS AND BEARINGS (DEVICES DESIGNED TO MINIMISE FRICTION OF MOTION BETWEEN FIXED AND MOVING BIKE PARTS). AS YOU MAY HAVE GATHERED BY NOW, THERE ARE A LOT OF MOVING PARTS ON A BICYCLE, AND A DROP OF OIL WILL GO A LONG WAY TO KEEP THEM MOVING SMOOTHLY.
- TIGHTEN ALL VISIBLE NUTS AND BOLTS SUCH AS THOSE ON YOUR RACKS, BRAKE LEVERS AND GEAR SHIFTERS.
- CHECK FOR ANY FRAYING BRAKE AND GEAR CABLES.
- GIVE YOUR BIKE A PROPER CLEAN USING LUBES AND DEGREASERS, BRUSHES AND SPONGES.

X NO-NOS

1. DON'T BE MR MUSCLE

When loosening and tightening various bicycle parts with a spanner, be gentle. Bike bits are usually made of lightweight materials, which are strong but not super-robust. So when tightening or loosening nuts and bolts, you should be firm (otherwise they'll fall off), but not too firm. Also remember the clockwise/anticlockwise rule. Which is: tighten in a clockwise direction; loosen in an anticlockwise direction.

2. DON'T FORGET TO CHECK YOUR LIGHTS

Otherwise, you'll have the law to deal with. The law in many countries states that cyclists must ride with a white light at the front and a red at the rear. Those in the know also recommend a flashing light, using a Light Emitting Diode (LED), but this can only be used in addition to the lights mentioned above (a fact that angers many cyclists). But note that in some countries it is illegal to attach a flashing light to your bike.

3. DON'T FALL OUT OF LOVE WITH YOUR BRAKES

Or you'll fall off your bike. Your brakes are the most safety-specific part of your bike and therefore need the most care and attention. Before setting off on a ride, always make sure that all the nuts and bolts are present and correct. Work a regular brakes checklist into your maintenance routine: once a week, make sure they're working correctly; once a fortnight, look at the pads; once a month, check lubrication and for any fraying cables.

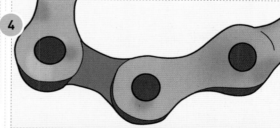

4. DON'T NEGLECT YOUR BIKE'S FEELINGS

If you're spending all that time on maintenance, don't do silly things like putting your bike to one side after a wet ride – otherwise, expect rust. Wait for the weather to brighten up, then take it on a short ride to expel any water from the bearings. If you do find a rusty nut or bolt, soak it in oil, then try and loosen it. Another thing not to forget is security. The heavy-duty D-lock is best. Run the lock through the frame and back wheel, remove the front wheel or lock it too, then attach the lock to something immobile like a lamppost.

Tyre Trouble

I t was all going so well. You were happily cycling down the road and then – oops! – a pothole appears or you ride over a shard of glass or something. In any case, you now have a flat. But don't feel deflated too. Unless it's a massive gash, punctures are easy to fix. Here's how . . .

WHAT TO DO

Before even tackling a puncture, if possible remove the wheel. This makes fixing a puncture easier. If you haven't got the necessary kit to hand, though, it's not compulsory.

Remove the tyre and tube:

1. Deflate the tyre and remove the valve nut (if your model has one).

2. Go to the opposite end of the wheel and work the tyre back and forth to free it from the rim.

3. Using the rounded end of the tyre lever, push it under the tyre bead, then yank it down to lift the bead over the rim.

4. Hook the lever end onto a spoke and, about 10cm (4in) around, repeat the process with a new tyre lever. Do this with three levers – you shouldn't need any more.

5. Now go round the tyre, prising the sidewall away from the rim with your thumb.

6. Remove one of the tyre levers and run it between the rim and tyre, lifting the remaining tyre over the rim wall.

7. One side of the tyre should now be free from the rim. Reach inside and coax out the tube.

Mend the puncture:

1. Check the tube for any obvious thorns or cuts in the tread.

2. Find the puncture. The easiest way to do this is to pump the tyre up before removing it and then listen for the telltale hiss. Alternatively, take the tube out, hold it underwater – use a nearby puddle, for instance – and look for any escaping bubbles.

3. Circle the puncture with the crayon/chalk so you don't lose it.

4. Rub the area around the puncture with emery paper to remove any dirt and help the glue to bond.

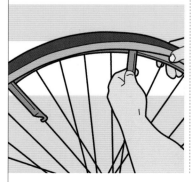

HOLEY WAR

Get far too many punctures? It could be that your tyres are simply worn out – get new ones then. Or it might be because you're not pumping your tyres up to the right pressure. Correct pressures should be between 2.1–3.4 bars (30–50psi) for mountain bikes, and between 6.2–8.3 bars (90–120psi) for 700C tyres on other bikes – consult your bike manual or dealer for precise figures. Check your pressure every fortnight.

DOMESTIC GOD

Carry a spare tube with you at all times. It won't take up much space and you never know when you'll need it. Also consider investing in a spare folding tyre, available from all good bike shops. This marvellous invention will fit snugly under your saddle. And what's more, it could save you from a long walk home.

5. Apply a thin coat of glue around the puncture.

6. Leave to dry.

7. Press the patch into position, with the centre bang on top of the puncture. Smooth it out, avoiding any air bubbles. Use the end of the tyre lever to press it down firmly.

Refit the tyre and tube:

1. Inflate the tube slightly.

2. Push the section of the tube with the valve stem into the tyre and the valve stem through its hole on the rim. Screw on the rim nut later.

3. Go round the wheel tucking the tube into the deepest part of the rim. Make sure it goes on evenly.

4. Next, starting at the valve, push the tyre bead over the edge of the rim. Do this all the way round the tyre. Hold the base of the valve stem clear of the rim as you do this, otherwise it might catch on the bead.

5. When the tyre is fitted neatly, pump it up.

6. Check the valve is upright, screw on the rim nut and spin the wheel.

7. Everything should be perfect now. If not, I'm sorry, but start again.

8. If the puncture has been mended – hurrah! You can now ride off into the sunset. But after three or more punctures, it might be worth replacing the tube. After all, you never know when one of the patches will pop off . . .

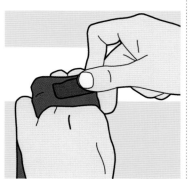
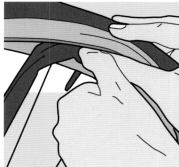
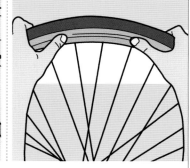

Ready, Steady . . . Go!
The Ten-minute Road Check

Do this as often as you can – it's best to know if something's wrong before setting out. Bikes can be a source of great joy and freedom but bear in mind you're more vulnerable than other road users. Keep your two wheeled machine in perfect nick though and you'll be a safer and more confident cyclist.

1 **Wheels and tyres:** Look for any cuts, debris and general wear. Ensure the tyres are inflated to the correct pressure. Spin them around to see if the wheels are running 'true'.

2 **Gears:** Turn the pedals and move through the gears – the chain should shift smoothly. Check the cables for fraying. On the rear mech, turn the jockey wheels; they shouldn't seize up. On the front mech, check the chain cage is parallel to the chain.

3 **Chain:** Turn the cranks backwards and look closely for any bent links.

4 **Cranks:** Check the crank bolts by holding one crank and trying to move the other. If there's any movement, tighten the bolts. Then remove the chain and make sure the cranks are running smoothly. Inspect the chainring bolts with an Allen key. Look down from above and see if the cranks and chainring are straight.

DOMESTIC GOD

Think about your pedals. You need good ones, yet most bike manufacturers will fob you off with the cheapest models possible. If yours don't seem up to scratch, replace them with pedals that have a decent cage and good bearings. Don't skimp on maintenance either; clean and lubricate regularly. Creaking pedals could mean the bearings in the crank are dry. Remove the pedal and grease the axle and its ball bearings.

5 **Headset:** Look for any cracks. Any wobbles between the forks and the frame mean the headset needs adjusting.

6 **Brakes:** Make sure they're properly adjusted. Squeeze the levers – the brakes should be fully on when you squeeze them halfway down. The brake pads should not be worn. The cables must not be frayed.

7 **Lights and reflectors:** Make sure your lights are working at full power. If you need to change a bulb, avoid touching the glass directly – use a piece of tissue or cloth to hold it in place.

8 **Frame:** Look for any cracks. Also check the saddle is secure.

Index

Alcohol   33
Aluminium   29
Aluminium Foil   27
Armpits   129
Ashes   66
Ashtrays   57

Bacteria   20, 23, 105
Barrons, Sir Richard   39
Bathroom   122-139
Bath, Cleaning of   129
Bed, Making of   107
Bedding   106-107
Bedroom   100-121
Beeton, Mrs   13
Belts   112
Bicarbonate of soda
                       20, 24, 27
Bidet   129
Bike   164-173
Bike Kit   166-167
Bills, Paying of   95
Bleach   44
Bleaching Symbols   43
Blinds   63
Blocked Drain   35
Blocked Sink   34-35
Boiling Water   17
Brake Fluid   155
Buck's Fizz   87
Burns   136
Business Cards   94
Button, Replacement of   110

Cables   93
Calories, Burning of
                6, 20, 31, 73, 131
Carbon Monoxide Detector   67
Car   142-163
Car Horn   144
Car Kit   146-147
Car Seat   145
Car, Exterior   142-143
Car, Interior   144-145
Champagne   87
Chewing Gum, Removal   48
Chicken, Carving   88-89
Chimney Care   66
Chocolate   33, 48
Chopping Board   22
Chore Chart:
  Bathroom   124
  Bedroom   102
  Bike   168
  Car   150
  Dining Room   78
  General   9
  Home Office   92
  Kitchen   14
  Living Area   56
  Utility Room   40
Cleaning Products   41
Closet   108
Clothes Labels   42
Clothes Pegs   46-47
Clothes   111-113
Clothes, Storage   108
Clutch Fluid   155
Cobwebs   63
Cockroaches   20
Cocktails   86
Coffee   24
Coloured Clothing   42
Compost   29
Computer, Cleaning of   93

Coolant   154
Corkscrew   87
Cotton   42
Cross-contamination   20
Crumb Test   58
Curtains   68
Cuts   136

Declutter   58, 94-95, 105
Defrosting   24
Delicates   42, 46
Detergents   44
Diet   33
Dining Room   76-89
Dinner Party   84
Dirty Dishes   57
Dirty Laundry   41
Dishwasher   21, 23
Discarded Clothes   57
DIY   34-35
Doona: see Duvet
Doormat   70
Drains   131
Dress Sense   112-113
Drying Clothes   46-47
Drying Rack   20
Drying Symbols   43
Dry Clean Symbols   43
Dry Cleaning   112
Dust Mites   60, 105
Dusting   60-61
Duvet   106, 107

Earache   136
Electric Fireplace   66
Ellis, A   101
Emergencies   35, 94
Essential Oils   132
Exfoliation   134

Eyebrows	126	Houseplants	96-97	Morris, William	55
Fabric Conditioner	44	Hygiene, Food	22	Mould: see Mildew	
Face Mask	132	Hygiene, Personal			
Face Scrub	132		126-127, 134-135		
Feather Duster	60, 61			Naked Cleaning	129
Filing	93, 94-95			Napkin Folding	82
Fireplace	66-67	Insect Bites	136	Nausea	136
Fire Laying	67	Insects	23	Newspaper	28, 125
Fire Surround	66	Ironing	50-52	No-nos:	
First Aid	136-137	Ironing Symbols	43	Bathroom	125
Five Portions	33			Bedroom	103
Floors	22, 70-71			Bike	169
Flower Arranging	83	Kitchen	12-37	Car	151
Food Facts	32-33	Kitchen Organisation	17	Dining Room	79
Food Hygiene	22	Kitchen Utensils	16-19	Fashion	112
Food Pyramid	32	Knives	17, 89	Home Office	93
Food Storage	31			Kitchen	15, 21
Food, Encrusted	20			Living Area	57
Food, Frozen	24	Lampshade	69	Pets	99
Foot Care	127	Larder	30	Utility	41
Foot Pedals	144	Laundry	41, 42-47	Nutrition	30-31
Freezers	24-25	Laundry Symbols	43		
		Leather Furniture	69		
		Leftovers	25, 89	Oil	154
Garage	140-173	Lemon Juice	17	Ovens and Hobs	27
Gearstick	145	Linen	42		
Glass	28	Living Area	54-75		
Glassware	85	Lost Sock Syndrome		Pampering	132-133
Goldfish	99		45, 107, 108	Paperwork	94-95
Guests	79, 84, 118-119			Pasta Server	19
				Pepper Mill (Huge)	18
		Magnetron	36	Personal Hygiene	
Hair Care	126	Mattress	106		126-127, 134-135
Handbrake	145	Meals, Serving	81	Pestle & Mortar	19
Hands	127	Medicines	137	Pets	21, 59, 98-99, 103
Handwashing	46	Menu Planning	79, 84	Pillows	104, 106
Hangover	136-137	Microwave	26, 36-37	Pizza Cutter	18
Headache	136	Mildew	45, 129	Plastic	28
Herb Chopper	18	Milk, Cheesy	25	Plunger	130
High Heels	71	Miniature Grater	18	Pockets, Emptying of	41
Home Office	90-99	Mirrors	128	Post	95

Power Cut	34	Starch	51	Washing Line	47
Pre-Washing	44	Steamer (Bamboo)	19	Washing Machine	42-45, 53
Puncture (Bike)	170-171	Steering Wheel	144	Washing Symbols	43
		Storage	58, 59	Washing Up	15, 20-21
		Stubble	127	Washing Walls	62-63
Questionnaire	7	Suitcase, Packing of	120-121	Washing (Car)	158-159
		Suits	112, 121	Windows	63
		Sweeping	73	Windscreen	156-157
Rampley-Sturgeon, Joanna		Swift, Robert	77	Wine, Red	87
	123	Synthetics	42	Wine, White	87
Recycling	28-29			Wiping	15, 62-63
Refrigerators	24-25			Wood	61
Relaxation	132-134	Table, Dressing	82-83	Wood-Burning Stove	66
Rewards	6	Table, Laying	80-81	Wooden Floors	71
Road Check (Bike)	172-173	Takeout, Reheating	37	Wooden Furniture	63
Road Check (Car)	162-163	Tea Towel	20	Wool	42, 46, 52, 108
Roberts, Mark	91	Teeth	127		
Routine	8, 22, 116-117	Toenails	103		
Rugs	71	Toilet Roll	103	Zipper, Stuck	111
		Toilet Seat	125		
		Toilet, Cleaning	131		
Safety	34-35	Toilet, Unblocking	130		
Sewing	110	Tool Box	148-149		
Sheets	107	Towels (Fluffy)	45		
Shoes	114-115	Towels (Wet)	45, 103, 131		
Shower, Cleaning of	129	Trash	15, 28		
Shutters	63	Troubleshooting (Car)	160-161		
Silverware	21	Tumble Dryer	46-47		
Sink	20, 34-35, 129	Tyre Pressure	152-153		
Skin, Shedding of	105				
Smoke Alarms	34, 67				
Soap	138-139	Upholstery, Care for	68		
Sofa	69	Utility Room	38-53		
Sofa Bed	69				
Sore Throat	136				
Spa	132-133	Vacuum Attachments	75		
Spaghetti Measurer	19	Vacuum Cleaner	74-75		
Stain Removal Kit	64	Vacuuming Techniques	72		
Stain Removal (Clothing)	48-49	Vegetarians	84		
Stain Removal (Floors)	64-65	Vinegar	23, 128, 129		
Stains	93	Washer Reservoir	157		